lls for Living

Group Counseling Activities for Young Adolescents

Rosemarie S. Morganett

Research Press
2612 North Mattis Avenue
Champaign, Illinois 61821

94 93 92 91 90 5 4 3 2

Copies of this book may be ordered from the publisher at the address given on the title page.

Cover design by Tino Stephanile
Composition by Circle Type Corp.

ISBN 0-87822-318-5
Library of Congress Catalog Number 89-61588

To Dr. Warren J. Valine
Auburn University
Mentor and Friend

CONTENTS

PREFACE

Designing, organizing, conducting, and evaluating a multisession counseling experience is a formidable task for a beginning counselor or even for the veteran counselor with little group experience. Over the past several years, I have discovered that getting started in group counseling is an accomplishment of large proportions and, if one only had a clear path to follow, the task would be much less difficult.

My purpose in writing this book is to offer school counselors and other mental health service providers uncomplicated guidelines for conducting skill-building group counseling activities for young adolescents. It is not my intention to provide an in-depth discussion of the issues involved in the group counseling process. Many excellent resources exist in this area, and to these the reader is referred for further study. What this book does do is briefly tell how to get the group counseling effort off the ground and present some basic guidelines for group success. In addition, it offers step-by-step group counseling agendas for eight different topic areas. These topics have been chosen because they address frequently occurring developmental needs and problems in young adolescents, as seen by school counselors and administrators and by mental health professionals working in child protective services, community counseling agencies, probation departments, and other service areas. Finally, appendixes provide sample forms and letters, a student selection checklist, pretests/posttests for each topic area, and ethical guidelines for group counselors devised by the Association for Specialists in Group Work.

It is my hope that this book will be the starting point from which to begin many successful group experiences. What counselors do best is enable others to use relationship, communication, and coping skills. This book is meant to help empower you in your endeavor.

ACKNOWLEDGMENTS

This book is the expression of 20 years of influence from the children, adolescents, and adults with whom I have worked and the many colleagues and graduate students from whom I continually learn. I deeply appreciate their support and stimulation.

Special gratitude goes to my husband, Lee Morganett, leader of my family group, whose patience and never-flagging encouragement kept me on task. Ann Wendel and Karen Steiner of Research Press have given expert advice and many hours of editing, and I thank them warmly and sincerely. Last, I deeply thank Dr. Warren J. Valine of Auburn University for his inspiring me to pursue groupwork as a specialty and for his continued nourishment of my career.

INTRODUCTION

The media daily chart the epidemic of serious problems that children and adolescents in our society must face: teenage suicide, substance abuse, divorce and relationship failures, career and value confusion, depression, and so forth. Although group counseling has had a relatively brief history as a technique for teaching coping skills, it is beginning to be recognized as a valuable approach in helping youth deal with such personal and interpersonal needs and conflicts (Dinkmeyer & Muro, 1979).

Why Group Counseling?

Counseling groups for young people provide an atmosphere of acceptance, encouragement, and safe experimentation for new behaviors. Children in our society learn, play, and socialize in groups—thus this medium can be readily used for the purpose of psychological education (Seligman, 1982). In addition, because peers strongly influence the young adolescent, group counseling enhances the possibility that youths will attempt new behaviors practiced and modeled by their peers and significant others (Gazda, 1989).

It is important in this regard to distinguish between group counseling and group guidance. Group guidance involves sharing information with a large group, perhaps an entire class. This type of information, which should be provided on a regular basis, can help students make better life decisions about such matters as use of drugs/alcohol, career paths, and so forth. Thus guidance deals primarily with cognitive content and is designed to prevent these areas from becoming problems. On the other hand, group counseling focuses primarily on feelings and the resolution of affective issues and is intended to help those students who are already having behavioral or personality problems. Although the group counseling approach is primarily remedial, in the sense that it can keep these difficulties from developing into more serious problems, it also serves a preventative purpose.

Group counseling is not a cure-all for all problems, nor is it for all counselors or all clients. Some youngsters need more intense, individualized help and would best be served by individual counseling or by family therapy. However, group counseling does offer a unique learning opportunity.

Organizing the Group Experience

Conducting a group counseling experience is a process that begins long before the first session and extends well beyond the last. The process described in the following pages will vary according to your own setting and circumstances—feel free to use what you need and omit what is superfluous. In general, however, getting a group counseling effort going involves the following major steps.

1. Conduct Needs Assessment
2. Develop Written Proposal
3. Advertise the Group
4. Obtain Informed Consent from Parent/Guardian
5. Conduct Pregroup Interview
6. Select Group Members
7. Administer Pretest
8. Conduct Sessions
9. Administer Posttest
10. Conduct Postgroup Follow-up and Evaluation

Step 1: Conduct Needs Assessment

The counselor has an initial obligation to find out what group services are needed by the clients in a particular setting. You will not be able to provide everything for everyone, but an initial needs assessment can help you focus your efforts. In addition, the information gained from the needs assessment can be useful in persuading administrators and teachers to offer their cooperation in allowing students to be released from class to attend group and their support in the form of materials, secretarial help, volunteers, equipment, and so forth. Finally, after the intervention has been conducted, the needs assessment can be used along with information from the postgroup evaluation to demonstrate accountability to the school administration, colleagues, parents, and group members.

The school counselor serves at least three major populations: students, faculty/administrators, and parents. Each of these populations is a valuable source of information regarding what types of services are needed and what problematic areas could be addressed by group counseling. A specific needs assessment could be conducted to determine what topics group counseling could address. The agendas in this book are examples of these sorts of topics: dealing with parental divorce, learning anger management skills, meeting and making friends, and so forth. One convenient way of conducting a specific needs assessment for group counseling would be to use simple survey forms like those illustrated in Appendixes 1 and 2.

A specific needs assessment can be undertaken as often as necessary. Generally, target problems will not change drastically within a year or two. However, a change in the environment or circumstances in your area may well create new needs. For instance, in one community, a large ship-building industry closed. Many students in two school districts were affected by their parents' loss of work, and acting-out behaviors and other problems increased as family tensions mounted. It was obvious without any formal assessment that students needed help dealing with this locally devastating situation, and counselors reacted quickly to provide appropriate group services.

Step 2: Develop Written Proposal

After you have determined that there is a need for a particular group counseling experience, the next step is to develop a written proposal detailing what you are going to do and how you are going to do it. Once you have the purpose and plan for your group on paper, you will feel more confident about actually getting started. In addition, a written proposal can help answer the many questions you can expect to receive from school administrators, teachers, colleagues, parents, and potential group members.

The written proposal should include the following types of information. [1]

1. Description and Rationale
    - What is your purpose in conducting the group?
    - Whose needs does it meet?
    - What kind of group will it be (skill building, personal growth, decision making, problem solving, etc.)?
    - What topics are going to be explored in the group?
2. Objectives
    - What objectives do you have in mind for this group?
    - Are your objectives reasonable for the age and abilities of the participants?
    - Are your objectives clear? Measurable? Reasonable for the length of counseling experience proposed?
3. Logistics
    - Who will lead the group? What are the leader qualifications?
    - Who will be responsible for making sure that ethical guidelines are followed?
    - How will group members be selected?
    - When will the group meet? If during regular class time, do all parties (teachers, students, parents) agree?
    - How many members will be selected, and what are the criteria for inclusion? Is there a plan to provide services for those who are not selected?
    - Where will the group meet, and for how long?
    - Will the group be closed or open to new members as the group progresses?
    - What will you do if members want to drop out?
4. Procedures
    - What kind of techniques will you be using? (Possibilities include relaxation, role playing, behavioral modeling, self-improvement exercises, self-reinforcement, etc.)
    - How and when will you explain the risks of being involved in a group?
    - How will you protect members from being hurt physically or psychologically?
    - Will you take special precautions because participants are legal minors?
    - How will you explain confidentiality and its limits?
    - How will you handle parents or others who might want you to divulge a child's confidences?

[1] These guidelines are based generally on recommendations provided by Gerald Corey and Marianne Schneider Corey in *Groups: Process and Practice* (3rd ed.), 1987, Monterey, CA: Brooks/Cole.

- How will you obtain informed consent from the group member and parents or guardian?
- Will you require both parents to sign an informed consent if there is a noncustodial parent?
- Are you using any recording devices or conducting any research?

5. Evaluation
   - How do you plan to determine whether a member has changed due to exposure to the group experience?
   - How are you going to determine whether your goals and objectives have been met?
   - What follow-up procedures do you anticipate?
   - Who will receive evaluation data about the group?
   - How will evaluation data be stored? Who will have access?
   - How do you plan to evaluate leader performance?

In addition to dealing with these general points, the proposal can include specific outlines for each group meeting. These outlines should spell out the exact goals, materials, and processes involved. The group agendas in this book provide one of many possible frameworks for organizing group content. Experiment with what works best for your situation.

Step 3: Advertise the Group

There are many ways of letting potential participants know about an upcoming group. A good place to start is with the individuals who have the most contact with your student population: administrators, teachers, and other counselors. (Parents, school nurses, and school psychologists are others who might also refer students.)

Administrators

After approval has been given for the group, you will want to let all of the school administrators know what will be happening. In many schools, the assistant principal sees students who are having academic or behavioral difficulties and will be in a position to refer or recommend candidates.

Teachers

You could choose to inform teachers about the upcoming group by making a brief announcement at a faculty meeting or by holding a "minimeeting" in the teachers' lounge before or after classes. A written handout can also be circulated to announce the group (see Appendix 3). If you have conducted a specific needs assessment with the faculty, teachers will probably already have heard of the group counseling effort and be more willing to make referrals.

Teachers' questions and concerns often center on the time the group is scheduled and arrangements for students to make up classwork they may miss. They are also likely to be interested in hearing about their students' progress in the group. When providing this kind of information, be sure not to jeopardize the youngsters' right to confidentiality.

Counselors

Your colleagues in the counseling department will be familiar with students who are having problems coping in different areas and will be a good source for referrals. Ask them to mention the group to the students and parents with whom they work. You or other counselors could also make a brief announcement about the group in homeroom classes to invite students to talk with you about membership. You can also post signs or use direct contact to let students know about the group.

Having enough members seems to be a major concern of beginning counselors or counselors in training. Actually, it is very common to find that you have many more applicants than you can include in the group. (If you have made the rounds to each homeroom to announce the group, you can probably expect a large number of self-referrals.)

Step 4: Obtain Informed Consent from Parent/Guardian

In many school corporations, parents or legal guardians must provide a written informed consent in order for minor children to participate in group counseling. Informed consent involves the provision of specific information about the group so that the client (and, in the case of the minor child, the parent/guardian) can make an intelligent decision about whether or not to participate. Cormier and Cormier (1985) have developed a general checklist for informed consent that incorporates the following points.

1. Description of each strategy, including activities involved
2. Rationale for or purpose of the strategy
3. Description of the therapist's role
4. Description of the client's role
5. Description of possible risks or discomforts
6. Description of expected benefits
7. Estimated time and cost of each strategy

8. Offer made to answer client's questions about strategy
9. Client advised of the right to discontinue strategy at any time
10. Explanations given in clear and nontechnical language
11. Summary and/or clarifications used to explore and understand client reactions (p. 306)

Corey and Corey (1987) have developed similar guidelines for what counseling clients have a right to expect.

1. A clear statement regarding purpose of the group, the procedures to be used, and the leader's policies and ground rules
2. A statement of the education and training of the leader
3. Clarification of what services can and cannot be provided within the group
4. A discussion of both the rights and responsibilities of being a group member
5. Reasonable safeguards to minimize the potential risks and hazards of the group
6. Respect for member privacy
7. Freedom from undue group pressure or coercion from either members or leaders to participate in exercises or to disclose matters they are unwilling to discuss
8. Protection against either verbal or physical assaults
9. Notice of any research involving the group, any observations of the group through one-way mirrors, or any audio or video taping of group sessions
10. Full discussion of the limits of confidentiality, including a statement from the leader concerning how information acquired during group sessions will be used outside the group structure (pp. 51–52)

Finally, Gazda (1989) points out that clients have a right to the following information about the group.

1. The procedures and basic approach to be used and why they will be used
2. The leader's role in the group's process
3. The members' roles in the group process and the risks they might incur should they join the group
4. Any discomforts that group members might experience
5. What group members can expect in the way of outcome(s) from engaging in the group process
6. What other methods are available that the group member might consider as an alternative to participating in the group
7. Assurance that group members can ask questions about the group process at any time
8. Assurance that group members can withdraw from the group at any time or refuse to participate or be a part of any portion of the group process (p. 302)

The importance of obtaining informed consent from the parent/guardian, as well as from the student, cannot be overstated. One good way to provide the necessary information is to use a letter and form like those illustrated in Appendixes 4 and 5. Your school may have a policy requiring a consent from both custodial and noncustodial parents; be sure to look into this matter before making any final selection of members.

Step 5: Conduct Pregroup Interview

The main purposes of the pregroup interview are (1) to obtain informed consent from the student, (2) to request the student's commitment, and (3) to obtain information that will be helpful in making a selection decision.

Interviewing each student who expresses an interest in becoming a member of the group can be quite complicated and time consuming. The TAP-In Student Selection Checklist (see Appendix 6) can help standardize and objectify the interview process. TAP stands for *Tell, Ask,* and *Pick;* the questions on this checklist thus help the counselor "tap-in" to the student's world.

In the interview, it is a good idea first to talk to students for a while about their expectations of the group and what their interests might be in participating. Then, before going through the checklist, you could say something like, "Being a member of a group is very special. There are a number of things I need to tell you and ask you, so I have them written down so I won't forget. OK?" It is especially important to use language the student can understand to describe what will be involved in the group.

Step 6: Select Group Members

One of the most critical factors in the preparation for group counseling is preselection of group members. (George Gazda, one of the founders of the Association for Specialists in Group Work, once said at a convention workshop that selection of members is 50 percent of what it takes to get your group to "fly.") Unfortunately, this point is often neglected by beginning group counselors.

Specific guidelines for selection are given for each group described in this book. Some general comments are in order here as well. First, each time you lead a group, there is the potential for tremendous personal growth in each student. There also exists the risk of personal harm for each student. Because of its many intertwining relationships, it is said that a group has a life of its own. Whatever happens to one member affects all members. Thus it is the responsibility of the leader to select participants who will be most likely to have positive experiences and to screen out those who are at risk for harm to themselves or others.

The factors of homogeneity and heterogeneity need to be considered in selecting group members who will work together smoothly. *Homogeneity* refers to selection on the basis of likenesses (e.g., youths who have all experienced a family divorce). The more alike the group members, the faster they will relate to one another and develop a sense of cohesion. Despite the value of homogeneity, *heterogeneity* is often the crucial ingredient in the success of the group counseling effort. Within a group homogeneous for the experience of divorce, you could select group members at different stages or who have different coping skills. For example, you might choose two members whose families experienced a divorce 2–3 years ago and who include stepparents or stepsiblings; two or three whose families have gone through a divorce during the last year; and two or three whose families are currently going through a divorce (assuming the prospective members are not in crisis). In this way, each group member will have others who are dealing with the same set of problems but who have different coping skills and perspectives.

School counselors can be under considerable pressure to select students for a group experience who all exhibit the same symptoms (e.g., youth who are truant, failing academically, acting-out, or aggressive). However, selecting an entirely homogeneous population is most likely to result in a negative group experience for both members and counselor. Rule number one in selection is that *each member needs other members from whom he or she can learn appropriate behaviors.* If all the members are engaged in the same negative behaviors, then positive models are not present and the value of working in the group is negated.

The following suggestions for selection are meant as broad guidelines only. Research in this area is inconclusive, so use them at your discretion to develop your own feelings on what works and what does not. [2]

Select

1. A range of participants so each student will have at least one positive behavioral model
2. Students who are no more than 2 years apart chronologically
3. Students with approximately the same social, emotional, intellectual, and physical maturity
4. Students who respond well to social influence
5. Students who work well in other group situations (e.g., teams or class projects)
6. Students of different racial, cultural, ethnic, and socioeconomic backgrounds, if possible
7. Students of both sexes unless the topic would cause one sex to be very uncomfortable (e.g., a male student in a group of pregnant females)

Do not select

1. Siblings or relatives who might feel they have to adhere to familial roles or expectations within the group
2. Students who are suicidal or homicidal, or who have seriously considered attempting either of these actions
3. Students who are involved in ongoing sexual activity (heterosexual or homosexual) if such behavior is exceptional within the peer group
4. Students who habitually lie or steal
5. Students experiencing an ongoing or recent crisis (unless the group is specifically geared to deal with this conflict)
6. Students whom you know or strongly suspect are being abused
7. Students whose parents are divided against having the child participate

[2] It is assumed that you are choosing members for a voluntary group. Involuntary groups are commonly found in residential child care or treatment centers, special school settings, and probationary situations. These situations present an entirely different set of counseling issues.

8. Students who are too "different" from the rest of the group (e.g., one pregnant student, one student from an ethnic minority, one student who is developmentally disabled, etc.)
9. Students who are extremely aggressive, either physically or verbally

Even though they might not be good candidates for a counseling group, students who fall into the "do not select" category are certainly still in need of services. You could work with these students individually or in a family group, or you could refer them to another counselor or to a mental health agency.

A final issue in selection concerns letting students know they have not been chosen. Even though it helps to mention clearly and frequently during the advertising and interviewing processes that not everyone who wants to be in the group can be included, some students may interpret not being selected as a significant adult rejection. If more groups on the topic are planned for later on, and the student is a genuine candidate, you could relate this information. Otherwise, individual counseling or referral may be the solution.

Step 7: Administer Pretest

A pretest and posttest can give valuable information about the group experience to the group leader, group members, and anyone else to whom the group leader might be accountable. Specifically, this information concerns whether an individual or the group as a whole has profited from the experience through a change in attitudes or behaviors.

If a main purpose of your group counseling activity is to conduct research, you will probably want to use a standardized instrument. On the other hand, if you would be satisfied with more general information about the group process, a counselor-constructed Likert-type scale like those provided for each of the groups in this book might be sufficient (see Appendix 7). It is important to point out that these measures are not sophisticated, normed instruments, nor are they meant to give proof of anything. However, these informal measures can allow you to estimate what might have happened as a result of the group experience. Another benefit of this approach is that it allows you to construct items to fit the goals and objectives of each session.

In addition to providing information about the impact of sessions on participants, the pretest can be used to help you select members for the group. For example, by administering a pretest designed to gauge test anxiety, you might be able to eliminate students whose test anxiety is in fact very low. It is important to point out, however, that self-report measures of this type are subject to inaccuracies. You might therefore want to augment the information from this measure with teacher and/or parent reports of test anxiety.

If the pretest is used as a screening tool, it could be administered during the pregroup interview to all students who wish to participate. If other selection criteria are used, the pretest could be given anytime after selection and before the first session.

Step 8: Conduct Sessions

The next step is to conduct the sessions. You can vary the number of sessions and their length to fit your topic and time schedule. Between 8 and 12 sessions are optimal in a school setting; fewer than 8 will not allow the dynamics of the group counseling process to unfold fully.

Step 9: Administer Posttest

After the group has ended, use the same instrument you used as a pretest for your posttest. It is important not to wait more than a week or two to give the posttest; if you do, you increase the chance that you are really measuring learning that has taken place since the group ended. You could reconvene the group a few days or a week later to do the posttesting, or you could have group members stop by the counseling office to complete the posttest privately. (The latter would help minimize the influence of peers on members' responses.)

Step 10: Conduct Postgroup Follow-up and Evaluation

Approximately 4–8 weeks after the last group session, some type of follow-up is appropriate. This session provides students with the opportunity to share their accomplishments and perceptions of what happened in the group and to get new ideas about how to continue working on issues raised in the group. It also offers an opportunity for students to support one another in reaching their behavior change goals, setting new ones, and overcoming obstacles. Encouragement and a renewal of commitment to work on behavior change are reinforcing and helpful.

The postgroup evaluation is essential for accountability and can be used for the following purposes.

1. For reporting to administrators, teachers, or parents the direction of change that may have occurred in the group as a whole as a result of participation

2. To compare pretest with posttest responses for each member to help that member achieve current and future goals
3. To obtain an idea of the effectiveness of the group leader
4. To provide information helpful in assisting group members with any problems that may have developed due to focusing on areas covered in the group
5. To assist the group leader in improving the group in the future

It is a good idea to write a brief report describing your experience and giving generalized data results from the pretest/posttest comparison. A two-page narrative and posting of means would be sufficient for most settings.

Be aware that the data from these tests belongs to the students taking the test and must be kept confidential. You might want to share general results with group members or others to whom you are accountable, but be sure to omit all identifying information.

Guidelines for Group Success

Counseling is both a science and an art. Although you can learn about and control many factors involved in the group process, many aspects are out of your control—and the process cannot be hurried. Nonetheless, knowing your content and following some basic guidelines can help your group experience be a successful one. This section deals with some of the mechanics and main considerations of the group counseling process.

Logistics

Some relevant logistical matters in conducting the group involve group size, scheduling of sessions, and the setting.

Group Size

The recommended number of students for group counseling involving preadolescents or adolescents is six to eight. This number allows each student to have an opportunity to participate actively and to express his or her ideas, needs, and feelings. If there are more than eight members, the shy or unassertive child will have less opportunity to become involved, and the leader may spend a great deal of time monitoring who is and who isn't participating rather than attending to other leadership functions. (A group of more than eight is best run by co-leaders.) On the other hand, if there are fewer than six members, the lack of different viewpoints and behaviors may cause the group to become too intense, with too much pressure on each student to participate.

Scheduling of Sessions

Gazda (1989) has surveyed the group counseling literature dealing with children and has concluded that the degree of disturbance of the participants should be used to determine the length and number of sessions, with 6 months to a year of weekly sessions being not uncommon for youngsters whose needs are great. Because devoting this much time to group counseling is an unrealistic goal in most schools, the group experiences included in this book have been limited to eight sessions of approximately 40–50 minutes each. These sessions can be expanded according to need or otherwise adapted to suit your particular circumstances.

It is recommended that you meet with the group once weekly. When planning the schedule, be sure to consider school vacation times: If you miss group one week, it may be difficult to regenerate the level of trust, cohesion, and commitment that members have developed so far.

Another issue relating to scheduling concerns the need to avoid causing students to be frequently absent from academic classes. One way of avoiding this conflict is to schedule the group sessions during a study hall or free period, or to use a different class period for each weekly session. In this latter situation, the first group session would be scheduled for the first period in the day, the second session for the second period, and so forth. Another way to keep the group from interfering with academic subjects is to schedule sessions during physical education classes, especially if the group topic is in some way related (e.g., stress reduction). It is much easier to support the psychological benefits of the group if participation does not put students at risk for academic distress.

Setting

In keeping with the serious nature of the confidentiality issue, it is recommended that you conduct group counseling in a setting where others will not be able to overhear what is said in the group. A room with a door that can be closed is best, and it is a good idea to post a "do not disturb" sign so no one will inadvertently walk in. If your own office is not big enough, perhaps an unused classroom, stage, administrator's office, or even storage room would be suitable.

To promote the personal growth of each individual, group members should sit in a circle that includes the leader's chair. Be sure that group members can see one another clearly. The circle will help students dispense with the notion that the leader is "in charge" and will help them learn to direct their comments to one another instead. Some topics (e.g., relaxation exercises) will lend themselves to having the group sit on blankets, mats, or beanbag chairs. Taking the group outside in nice weather is also an appealing possibility; however, this would not be a good idea if distractions such as a nearby physical education class or recess would interfere with the group's work.

Session Organization and Content

Each group session outlined in this book is divided into three parts: an *ice breaker* or *review, working time,* and *closing time.* The very first session of each group experience begins with an ice breaker, an activity designed to introduce students to one another and to encourage trust and cohesion. Spend as much time as needed on this activity in order to establish a norm of comfort and pleasure in coming to group. To increase continuity, subsequent sessions in each group begin with a review of the content of the preceding session.

Working is the term used in group counseling for the psychological business that is conducted. In the session agenda, the working time provides information members need to know and, generally, an activity to help members interact and learn new skills.

Finally, the closing time is designed to help students achieve a sense of completion about the group's work for the session and to allow them to leave the group with some degree of cognitive and affective comfort. Some session topics are related to heavy emotional issues, and the closing time gives group members an opportunity to share any unresolved feelings before returning to their regular school activities.

Many of the sessions involve self-improvement exercises for students to perform between sessions. These exercises (sometimes called *personal homework*) give students the opportunity to practice new ways of behaving outside the group, thus promoting transfer and generalization of what they have learned in the sessions. It is a good idea to have students repeat the rationale for doing any given self-improvement exercise in their own words. Being sure they are clear on the reasons for following through will help improve compliance.

Group Norms

One of the leader's most important roles is to help establish positive norms for expression and conduct in the group. One set of norms, *ground rules,* consists of explicit (generally written) statements concerning behaviors and issues that affect the group. These statements are developed by the leader and are added to by the members, usually at the first session. It is important that members be allowed to have some input into the creation of these rules so that they develop "ownership" of them and will be more willing to abide by them. The confidentiality rule is an especially important norm; others include such matters as being on time, allowing everyone to have a chance to talk, and the freedom to decline participation, if desired.

Other norms are unwritten, but no less important. The leader has a special role in developing the norms of a group because of his or her position as a behavioral model. For example, if the leader comes to group late and unprepared, then the members will tend to do so also, even if an explicit ground rule states that they are expected to arrive on time. If the leader gives positive feedback and praises students' successes and work, then members will also tend to be supportive and positive. If the leader lets everyone know through his or her behavior that it is OK to discuss feelings in the group, then members will begin to do so even if the leader has not explicitly stated that feelings will be discussed in group. Be aware of emerging norms in your group so that you can support positive norms and eliminate negative ones.

Group Dynamics

Although the topic of group dynamics cannot be discussed comprehensively here, a couple important aspects should be mentioned. The first is *trust,* the most essential ingredient in any relationship and the most important dynamic in groupwork. Without trust, there will be no involvement, movement, or growth. Because of learning in past relationships, people do not automatically trust one another. The students in your group will have had diverse experiences and will range from being completely untrusting to overly trusting. The trust level in the group needs to be nurtured and encouraged. Be patient and accepting of members' lack of trust because only with understanding and encouragement will they develop trust in you and in one another. Use modeling to help develop trust in the group: Trust yourself and trust members to work problems and issues out in a satisfactory manner. Your efforts will pay off in the long run.

A second important aspect of group dynamics, *cohesion,* has been called a feeling of "we-ness," a sense of being a group working toward a goal, or the desire within the group that propels it forward. More specifically, cohesion is the bond that unites members. In the beginning of a group, there will likely be little cohesion because members will be "fending for themselves." After doing activities together, discussing behaviors, and sharing feelings, ideas, and values, a sense of cooperation will begin to develop. You can tell if your group is becoming more cohesive because members will begin to change their behaviors. For example, they will be more likely to share personal feelings, trust others, come to group without being reminded, and take personal responsibility for doing self-improvement exercises. Like trust, cohesion can be enhanced by modeling: Allow members to participate on their own levels and be open about anxieties and concerns.

Leadership Issues

Among the most important leadership issues involved in the group experience are the personhood of the counselor, leadership style, and the decision whether or not to use a co-leadership model.

Personhood of the Counselor

Group counseling requires that the leader share aspects of his or her own *personhood* (personal behavior, attitudes, and feelings) with members. For this reason, it is neither possible nor desirable to be one thing in the counseling session and something different outside of it. All of us have areas where we are not using our potential to the fullest. If a counselor purports to be a model for young adolescents, then that counselor needs to be striving to be as authentic a person as possible. As Gerald Corey (1985) states in his text *Theory and Practice of Group Counseling*, "the most effective group direction is found in the kind of life the group members see the leader demonstrating and not in the words they hear the leader saying" (p. 39). Many other experts in the field have expressed similar opinions regarding the personhood of the counselor (e.g., Carkhuff & Berenson, 1977; Rogers, 1980; Yalom, 1975). The counselor's knowledge of procedures, activities, and evaluation methodology are certainly important, but the lifelong journey to developing one's potential remains the counselor's most important long-term task.

Leadership Style

Group leadership can be thought of in terms of a continuum of control over the group. At one end of this continuum is *leading*, or complete control over what is presented to and expected of group members. As in a lecture class, the leader presents the agenda and carries out the activities. Because group counseling is different from teaching, the recommended style of leadership is more toward the other end of the continuum, which involves shared leadership responsibilities. This style is frequently referred to as *facilitation*.

The facilitative approach encourages members to learn to take responsibility for themselves and respects members' ability to work out their own problems with the support, encouragement, and guidance of the counselor. However, this style can be scary for counselors who have used a very direct approach in their counseling work or who may have had many years of teaching experience. Leaders with this kind of background may be disinclined to give up their control of the group's agenda, but allowing members to learn personal responsibility for the direction of the group sessions can be an important stepping stone toward their transferring that knowledge outside the group.

A moderate amount of control over the group's agenda and process seems to work best. You may find that in the beginning sessions you are more inclined to adopt a leadership approach. As sessions progress, you will likely find your control relaxing as you begin to operate closer to the facilitative model. The younger your population, the more you will need to provide structure. However, even young children can benefit from the opportunity to be responsible for their own behavior change.

Co-leadership

Another aspect of leadership concerns whether one or two leaders will be involved. Although using two counselors to conduct one group may be impractical or prohibitively expensive, doing so has a number of distinct advantages, among them the opportunity to share knowledge, expertise, and feedback about the group process and the fact that co-leadership provides two behavioral models for the group. The co-leadership model may be essential in groups including more than eight students.

Ethical Issues

Although a complete discussion of the complex matter of ethics in group counseling is beyond the scope of this book, it is important to point out that the counselor who provides services for young adolescents has a responsibility to adhere to ethical practice even greater than that of a counselor working with adults. Ethical behavior is complicated because the counselor has not only a responsibility for his or her clients, but also for these clients' parents, the school administration, and society as a whole. Providing service is a question of serving many masters at once while keeping in mind the complex issues associated with confidentiality, participant rights, and psychological and physical risk.

The ethical guidelines developed by the Association for Specialists in Group Work are reprinted as Appendix 8 in this book. Before undertaking a group, leaders will want to review these guidelines and investigate the recommendations of any other professional organizations to which leaders may belong. It will also be helpful to review discussions of ethical responsibility found in various other group counseling resources (e.g., Corey, Corey, & Callanan, 1982; Cormier & Cormier, 1985; Gazda, 1989).

References and Recommended Reading

Carkhuff, R. R., & Berenson, B. G. (1977). *Beyond counseling and therapy* (2nd ed.). New York: Holt, Rinehart & Winston.

Corey, G. (1985). *Theory and practice of group counseling* (2nd ed.). Monterey, CA: Brooks/Cole.

Corey, G., & Corey, M. S. (1987). *Groups: Process and practice* (3rd ed.). Monterey, CA: Brooks/Cole.

Corey, G., Corey, M. S., & Callanan, P. (1982). *A casebook of ethical guidelines for group leaders.* Monterey, CA: Brooks/Cole.

Cormier, W. H., & Cormier, L. S. (1985). *Interviewing strategies for helpers* (2nd ed.). Monterey, CA: Brooks/Cole.

Dinkmeyer, D. C., & Muro, J. J. (1979). *Group counseling: Theory and practice* (2nd ed.). Itasca, IL: Peacock.

Donigian, J., & Malnati, R. (1987). *Critical incidents in group therapy.* Monterey, CA: Brooks/Cole.

Duncan, J. A., & Gumaer, J. (1980). *Developmental groups for children.* Springfield, IL: Charles C Thomas.

Gazda, G. M. (1989). *Group counseling: A developmental approach* (4th ed.). Boston: Allyn & Bacon.

Gazda, G. M., Asbury, F., Balzer, F., Childers, W., & Walters, R. (1977). *Human relations development: A manual for educators* (2nd ed.). Boston: Allyn & Bacon.

Gladding, S. T. (1988). *Counseling: A comprehensive profession.* Columbus, OH: Merrill.

Jacobs, E. E., Harvill, R. L., & Masson, R. L. (1988). *Group counseling strategies and skills.* Monterey, CA: Brooks/Cole.

Johnson, J. (1977). *Use of groups in schools: A practical manual for everyone who works in elementary and secondary schools.* Lanham, MD: University Press of America.

Jourard, S. (1968). *Disclosing man to himself.* New York: Van Nostrand Reinhold.

May, R. (Ed.). (1961). *Existential psychology.* New York: Random House.

Napier, R. W., & Gershenfeld, M. K. (1981). *Groups: Theory and experience* (2nd ed.). Boston: Houghton Mifflin.

Rogers, C. (1980). *A way of being.* Boston: Houghton Mifflin.

Seligman, M. (1982). *Group psychotherapy and counseling with special populations.* Baltimore: University Park Press.

Yalom, I. D. (1975). *The theory and practice of group psychotherapy* (2nd ed.). New York: Basic.

Group Agendas

Dealing with a Divorce in the Family

Some estimates indicate that between one-third and one-half of all children born in the 1970s will live in a family experiencing separation and divorce (Wallerstein & Kelley, 1980). Half of the divorces that occur involve minor children, with over one million youth affected each year by divorce (U.S. Census Bureau, 1989). Although there is some support for the fact that not all youngsters are adversely affected by divorce, there is also overwhelming evidence that the stress of a divorce can have negative effects on the academic, social, and emotional development of many (Glenn & Kramer, 1985; Wallerstein, 1984). Indeed, the experience of parental divorce can be the most devastating crisis a young adolescent must face.

The impact of divorce appears to be the most severe for young children, due to their lack of coping skills, inability to utilize outside support, and tendency to blame themselves for the situation (Wallerstein & Kelley, 1980). As youths approach adolescence, they develop a greater capacity for coping. However, if they already have academic and social problems (e.g., shyness, developmental disabilities, poor impulse control, etc.) or come from families experiencing discord, they remain at risk for further psychological problems.

Support from school and mental health professionals can attenuate the negative effects of divorce on youth (Gazda, 1989), and a growing body of research has found group counseling for children and adolescents experiencing a divorce in the family to be beneficial (e.g., Green, 1978; Hammond, 1981; Kessler & Bostwick, 1977; Omizo & Omizo, 1987; Titkin & Cobb, 1983). Activity groups and skills training components in group counseling for young adolescents have been especially recommended by such experts as Corey (1987) and Gazda (1989).

Group Objectives

1. To help students understand their own feelings about the divorce, as well as those of other family members
2. To promote understanding of the words, names, and living situations associated with the divorce/remarriage situation
3. To point out the diversity of beliefs about divorce and to help students clarify what they believe about it
4. To allow students to reenact and better integrate situations that might be causing them distress
5. To help students learn to identify their positive characteristics and share both positive and negative thoughts and feelings

Selection and Other Guidelines

The following target signs may indicate that a student is a candidate for this particular group experience.

1. Reverting to the behaviors of earlier developmental levels (e.g., whining, attention seeking, demanding, or sulking)
2. Changes in eating and sleeping patterns
3. Isolating self from family or others
4. A drop in grades or lack of motivation to complete homework or class assignments
5. Social aggression (starting fights with friends, siblings, or adults)
6. Hiding, avoiding, seeming "tuned out," or expressing dependency, daydreaming, or hostile behaviors

In addition to following the general selection criteria outlined in the Introduction, it is best to select students whose parents have separated or divorced over differing periods of time (in other words, a group homogeneous with respect to divorce but heterogeneous for the stage of dealing with divorce). A good mix would be two or three members whose parents have divorced recently, two or three with a 6- to 12-month history of parental separation, and two or three whose parents have been divorced for several years and/or have remarried.

Obtaining permission for the student's participation from both custodial and noncustodial parents is recommended and, in some cases, required. Doing so improves the chances that parents will support their child's learning about divorce; in addition, it demonstrates to students that the group organizers respect both parents and encourage open family communciation.

References and Recommended Reading

Allers, R. D. (1982). *Divorce, children, and the school.* Princeton, NJ: Princeton.

Corey, M. S., & Corey, G. (1987). *Groups: Process and practice* (3rd ed.). Monterey, CA: Brooks/Cole.

Dinkmeyer, D., McKay, G. D., & McKay, J. L. (1987). *New beginnings: Skills for single parents and stepfamily parents* (Leader's Manual, Parent's Manual, and Videotape). Champaign, IL: Research Press.

Einstein, E. (1982). *The stepfamily: Living, loving, and learning.* New York: Macmillan.

Gazda, G. (1989). *Group counseling: A developmental approach* (4th ed.). Boston: Allyn & Bacon.

Glenn, N. D., & Kramer, K. K. (1985). The psychological well-being of adult children of divorce. *Journal of Marriage and the Family, 47,* 905–912.

Green, B. J. (1978). Helping children of divorce: A multi-modal approach. *Elementary School Guidance and Counseling, 13,* 31–45.

Hammond, J. M. (1981). Loss of the family unit: Counseling groups to help kids. *Personnel and Guidance Journal, 59,* 392–394.

Kessler, S., & Bostwick, S. H. (1977). Beyond divorce: Coping skills for children. *Journal of Clinical Child Psychology, 6,* 38–41.

Omizo, M., & Omizo, S. (1987). *Children and adults of divorce: Group intervention strategies.* Paper presented at the Annual Hawaii Association for Counseling and Development Conference, Honolulu.

Rofes, E. (1982). *The kids' book of divorce.* New York: Random House/Vintage.

Titkin, E. A., & Cobb, C. (1983). Treating post-divorce adjustment in latency age children: A focused group paradigm. *Social Work with Groups, 4,* 15–28.

U.S. Census Bureau (1989). *Statistical abstract of the United States 1989* (109th ed.). Washington, DC: U.S. Government Printing Office.

Wallerstein, J. S. (1984). Children of divorce: Ten year follow-up of children. *American Journal of Orthopsychiatry, 54,* 444–458.

Wallerstein, J. S., & Kelley, J. B. (1980). *Surviving the breakup: How children and parents cope with divorce.* New York: Basic.

Getting Started

Goals

1. To help students become acquainted and begin to feel comfortable in the group setting
2. To choose appropriate ground rules for the group sessions
3. To identify why students want to be a part of the group and what they hope to learn
4. To promote understanding of the feelings family members may have when parents are divorcing
5. To recognize the potentially positive side of the new family situation

Materials

Construction paper in assorted colors
Marking pens in assorted colors
Sample Hand Name Tag (marked with the leader's own self-disclosures)
Straight pins
Chalkboard or chart paper

Process

Ice Breaker

1. Welcome students and briefly describe the goals of the group in general as well as this session in particular.
2. Distribute the art materials and show students the Sample Hand Name Tag (prepared before the session begins) to introduce the task. Instruct each student to use a marking pen to outline his or her hand on a piece of construction paper. Students then write their names in large letters on the palm of the hand and, on each finger, something they would like to share with the others, such as hobbies, siblings, special talents, and so on. When complete, give each student a straight pin to pin on the tag.
3. Begin modeling self-disclosure by discussing what is on your own Hand Name Tag. Ask students to share what is on their tags, as well as what they hope to learn from the group.

Working Time

1. Introduce the idea of ground rules, pointing out that rules help everyone be respected and have time to talk. Suggest a few basic ground rules, such as the following.
   - What we say and do here is private and stays in the group (confidentiality rule).
   - Everyone has the right to "pass"—that is, not to participate in an activity or part of an activity.
   - No fighting or arguing.
   - Each person gets time to talk.
   - When someone is talking, everyone else will listen.
2. Ask students to think of other ground rules for the group. List all rules on the chalkboard or on chart paper.
3. Discuss how living in a family in which parents are divorcing is a little like being in a storm: Things are moving fast, and the situation feels out of control. Family members have many strong feelings, and sometimes they express these feelings in different ways. For example, you could feel angry and left out of important things that are happening, helpless to do anything about what is going on, or lonely and miss one of your parents who has moved away. Discuss what it is like for students to have these feelings and what they would like to do to feel better about the divorce.

4. Introduce the idea that most situations, even negative situations, have some positive aspects. For example, after parents divorce you might have more attention from your dad, a new stepbrother or stepsister to be friends with, or better communication with your mom. Invite students to think of positive things they may have experienced as a result of the divorce.

Closing Time

1. Say something positive about each student. For example: "Jamie, you shared some painful things with us today, and we appreciate your letting us know how you feel" or "Lee, your idea for a ground rule will be a big help to us."
2. Ask whether there is anything anyone would like to say before the group ends and mention the topic of the next session (how divorce sometimes means the addition of new members to a family). Remind students of the confidentiality rule and the time for the next meeting.

What Do I Call My New Family?

Goals

1. To help students become aware of changes in words and names associated with the divorce/remarriage situation
2. To assist students in becoming more comfortable expressing such information to others
3. To illustrate that other group members also have new people in their families and have similar stresses in getting along

Materials

Drawing paper
Marking pens in assorted colors

Process

Review

1. Ask students to respond to the following sentence stems, then discuss their responses.
   - Having new people in my family makes me feel . . .
   - What I like best/least about having a stepmom/stepdad is . . .
   - Since the divorce I feel more . . .
   - I feel happy when my . . . does/says . . .
   - I'm angry when . . .
   - I'm sad when . . .
   - What I think about my parents' divorce is . . .

Working Time

1. Briefly describe the goals of the session.
2. Explain the idea that, when a parent remarries, new relationships exist between family members. For example:
   - The father and mother to whom you were born are your *biological parents,* even if you aren't living with them.
   - If your father remarries, the person he is married to is your *stepmother* or *stepmom.*
   - If your mother remarries, the person she is married to is your *stepfather* or *stepdad.*
   - Your stepfather's or stepmother's children are called your *stepbrothers* or *stepsisters.*
   - If your biological mother or father has children with your stepfather or stepmother, the children are your *half-brothers* or *half-sisters.*
3. Pass out the art materials and ask students to draw the people who live in their house and the persons who live with the biological parent with whom they do not live. Ask students to write each person's proper relationship under his or her picture, as illustrated on the next page.
4. Have students introduce their family members and tell each person's name and his or her correct relationship.
5. Discuss the following questions.
   - What did you learn about names when two families are merged together?
   - How do you think this information will be helpful to you?
   - Has anyone in your family gotten angry because they were called the wrong relationship name? Why do you think this might have happened?
   - Is it hard or easy for you to get along with the new people in your family?

My New Family

Biological Mom

Stepdad Mike

Stepbrother Aaron

Biological Dad

Stepmom Sharon

Half-sister Carrie

Closing Time

1. Invite students to think about these relationship names over the next week and to use them when and if the opportunity arises.
2. Ask whether there is anything anyone would like to say before the group ends and mention the topic of the next session (different living arrangements that occur when parents divorce). Remind students of the confidentiality rule and the time for the next meeting.

A New Place to Live

Goals

1. To point out the diversity of living arrangements resulting from a divorce and to suggest that such different living arrangements are all right
2. To help students learn that being flexible is part of growing up
3. To allow students to see that they can still be loved regardless of the change in their external circumstances

Materials

Drawing paper

Marking pens in assorted colors

Tape

Process

Review

1. Ask students whether they had the opportunity to use the information they learned in Session 2 about relationship names. Encourage them to discuss their experiences.

Working Time

1. Briefly describe the goals of the session.
2. Invite students to describe their different living situations. Some students may live in two places, with a custodial parent and a noncustodial parent. Others may have a parent who has moved a long distance away and have only one "home base." Still others may live with a grandparent or other family member.
3. Distribute the art materials and ask students to draw a picture of the house or apartment where they live most of the time. Then have them draw the floor plan of their room in this house, including furniture and some of their favorite possessions (e.g., basketball, pair of jeans, stereo). If they stay at another house or apartment part of the time, they could do another drawing for it.
4. Ask students to tape their pictures to the wall or chalkboard. Let them walk around and look at one another's pictures up close.
5. As a group, discuss the different types of living arrangements. The following questions may be helpful.
    - Would any of you be willing to tell about your picture? (Stress that students can share only what they want.)
    - Do you think it is hard to live in two places? If so, what makes it hard?
    - What kinds of rules do you have where you live? (Examples of rules include where students can go by themselves, how late they can stay out, what friends they can see, how much money they can spend, etc.)
    - What happens if you have two different sets of rules?
    - Would your family be living in a different house if you were any different than you are?
    - How do your parents show you they love you, even if they live in different houses?

Closing Time

1. Ask whether there is anything anyone would like to say before the group ends and mention the topic of the next session (people's ideas about divorce). Remind students about the confidentiality rule and the time for the next meeting.

Ideas about Divorce

Goals

1. To illustrate a wide range of beliefs about divorce and to help students clarify what they believe about it
2. To help students learn that it is all right for people to have different views
3. To show that, even though many kids believe they are the cause of their parents' divorce, in fact they are not

Materials

Divorce Ideas Scale

Process

Review

1. Ask students what the most important thing is they have learned so far in the group. Point out that different people have different ideas about what is most important.

Working Time

1. Briefly describe the goals of the session.
2. Explain that people also have very different ideas or values about divorce, then hand out copies of the Divorce Ideas Scale. Students may either complete the scale by themselves, or you may read the scale items aloud and have students raise their hands to indicate how they feel about each statement.
3. Go through the scale items one at a time and ask students to share their responses. Allow ample time for comments and discussion on each item, stressing that it is OK for people to feel differently about the divorce situation.
4. Ask students whether they have ever tried to change anything about themselves. (Examples might include studying harder to get better grades, improving grammar, or stopping fighting with a brother or sister.) Discuss how difficult it is to change one's own thoughts and behaviors, then ask students whether they think it is really possible to change someone else's thoughts and behaviors. Point out that we can only be responsible for ourselves. Therefore, we can't really be the cause of anyone else's thoughts or behaviors, including our parents' divorce.

Closing Time

1. Ask whether there is anything anyone would like to say before the group ends and mention the topic of the next session (expressing feelings about the divorce). Remind students of the confidentiality rule and the time for the next meeting.

Name______________________________ Date________________

Divorce Ideas Scale

Instructions: Circle or check the way you feel about divorce at this time.

1. Divorce is an awful, terrible thing.

   never sometimes most of the time always

2. When people marry, they should never get divorced.

   _____ I agree—they should never get divorced.

   _____ I think sometimes it's OK for them to get divorced.

   _____ I think it's OK for them to get divorced.

   _____ I think they should get divorced if they fight a lot and don't love each other anymore.

3. Things get better after a divorce.

   never sometimes most of the time always

4. Parents should not get married again after a divorce.

   _____ I agree—they should not get married again.

   _____ I think sometimes it's OK for them to marry again.

   _____ I think it's OK for them to get married again.

   _____ I think they should always get married again.

5. When parents get divorced, kids should be allowed to live with the parent they choose.

   never sometimes most of the time always

6. My stepparent loves me and treats me nice.

   never sometimes most of the time always

7. Stepbrothers or stepsisters can be fun.

   never sometimes most of the time always

8. Divorce is better than having Mom and Dad fighting all the time.

   never sometimes most of the time always

9. Divorce can be the kids' fault.

   never sometimes most of the time always

10. You should tell your teachers about it if your parents divorce.

    never sometimes most of the time always

11. How I feel right now about the divorce is . . .

    terrible not good I can deal with it very good

Expressing My Feelings

Goals

1. To help students become aware of their right to express both positive and negative feelings
2. To point out the need to express feelings honestly in relationships
3. To provide students with practice in expressing feelings in the group

Materials

Feelings Chart

Process

Review

1. Have students complete the following sentence stems, then discuss.
   - What I have learned so far about divorce is . . .
   - What I have learned about myself is . . .
   - What I have learned about other members of the group is . . .
   - What I feel better about is . . .

Working Time

1. Briefly describe the goals of the session.
2. Have students sit on the floor in a circle, backs toward the center and feet straight out. Make the circle small enough so that members are sitting close together.
3. Explain that the students are sitting in a Responsibility Circle, which teaches that our feelings are our own and that no one forces us to feel a certain way. Ask each student to tell how he or she feels that day and add at the end "and I take responsibility for my feeling."
4. Model the process. For example: "I feel sad today because our dog ran away over the weekend, and I take responsibility for my feeling." Invite each student to share.
5. Next, pass out a copy of the Feelings Chart to each student. Explain that we don't learn very much about feelings in school, so we may grow up not knowing very many names for feelings or not knowing how to express feelings. Point out that the Feelings Chart shows several major feelings in three different intensities. For example, if you are angry you could be just *annoyed.* If you are moderately mad, perhaps you are *aggravated.* If you are very mad, perhaps you are *furious.*
6. Stress that feelings are natural and that, if we keep feelings inside, we end up not sharing a very important part of us. It is just as important to express negative feelings like anger, hurt, and loneliness as it is to express friendship, love, and happiness. If we bottle up our negative feelings, they may make us act resentful and "turned off" in relationships.
7. Point out that one of the ways to deal with negative emotions is to be honest about them when they are fairly mild in intensity. Ask the group to consider the following story.

   Your dad says he will pick you up at 8:00 a.m. Saturday morning, so you get up early to be ready. Eight o'clock comes and goes, 9:00 comes and goes, then 10:00, but no Dad. At first, you are eager for him to come, then you wonder if he forgot, then you begin to get irritated that you got up so early for nothing. As the time passes, you get more and more angry, but you don't say anything to anyone—you just watch TV. Finally, at 3:00 p.m., he arrives. He says he forgot when it was he said he would pick you up. By this time, you are furious because the whole day seems wasted, but you still don't say anything—you just go along with him.

8. Discuss the following questions.
   - What do you think happens to furious feelings that don't get expressed? *(They stay inside.)*
   - What would happen if you could express your feelings as they occurred, when they were still manageable?
   - What would it be like if you expressed your feelings to your parents?
9. Explain that one way you can express your feelings is to use the formula *I feel/because.* For example: "I *feel* delighted that I can share this information with you today *because* I know it will help you cope better with your situation at home." Have each student practice this formula in the group by choosing a word from the Feelings Chart and saying why he or she feels that way.

Closing Time

1. Ask students whether they would be willing to use the *I feel/because* formula sometime before the next session. Stress that, even though they may not always get a positive response, it is important to tell the people who love you about your positive and negative feelings.
2. Ask whether there is anything anyone would like to say before the group ends and mention the topic of the next session (understanding how other people feel about the divorce). Remind students of the confidentiality rule and the time for the next meeting.

Feelings Chart

Happiness	Sadness	Anger	Love and Friendship	Fear	Distress
		High level of feeling			
elated	miserable	fuming	adoring	dreadful	anguished
giddy	crushed	furious	devoted	panicky	disgusted
overjoyed	worthless	outraged	passionate	horrified	speechless
radiant	humiliated	incensed	amorous	terrified	tormented
ecstatic	depressed	burned up	tender	petrified	sickened
jubilant	helpless	hateful	ardent	desperate	afflicted
		Moderate level of feeling			
tickled	forlorn	disgusted	caring	alarmed	badgered
glowing	burdened	irritated	dedicated	fearful	bewildered
excited	slighted	aggravated	generous	jittery	confused
joyous	abused	biting	loving	strained	disturbed
bubbly	defeated	hostile	empathic	shaky	impaired
delighted	dejected	riled	considerate	threatened	offended
		Low level of feeling			
amused	resigned	peeved	warm	uneasy	silly
cheerful	apathetic	bugged	amiable	tense	foolish
pleased	blue	annoyed	civil	timid	unsure
relieved	gloomy	ruffled	polite	anxious	touchy
glad	ignored	nettled	giving	nervous	lost
serene	glum	cross	kindly	puzzled	disturbed

Everyone Has Problems

Goals

1. To help students understand other family members' thoughts and feelings about the divorce situation
2. To allow students to reenact and better integrate situations that might be causing them distress

Materials

Several items of adult clothing (shoes, gloves, hats, purses, etc.)
Several items belonging to students (sweaters, jackets, notebooks, etc.)
Role Play Situations List

Process

Review

1. Ask whether anyone tried the *I feel/because* formula during the past week. Invite students to share their experiences expressing positive and negative feelings.
2. Extend the discussion to cover divorce in general by asking the following questions.
   - Have any of your own feelings or beliefs about divorce changed since the group started? If so, why do you think this has happened?
   - Why do you think we all have different ideas about what happens in a divorce?

Working Time

1. Briefly describe the goals of the session.
2. Explain that the group will get in touch with how other family members might experience the divorce by *role playing,* or acting out other people's "parts" in the family.
3. Hand out copies of the Role Play Situations List and ask for volunteers to play the parts in the first example. Allow volunteers to select an item of clothing or other article to represent their character. (Encourage students to choose a role different from their own in real life.)
4. Have the volunteers enact the role play. The other students are to observe and comment when the role play is complete. The following discussion questions may be helpful.

   To the volunteers
   - What did you like and dislike about playing your part?
   - What did you learn from changing roles?
   - What do you think the person you played was feeling or thinking?
   - What do you think the other people in the role play were feeling or thinking?

   To the observers
   - Do you think the role play showed a situation that could really have happened?
   - Has anything similar to this situation happened in your family? If so, how did you feel about it?
5. Follow the same procedure for the other role plays, discussing each as it is completed and giving all students a chance to act out a part.

Closing Time

1. Thank students for doing a good job on the role plays. Stress that everyone involved with a divorce has strong feelings that need to be expressed. Invite students to try to understand what another family member is thinking and feeling and let that person know they understand his or her point of view.
2. Ask whether there is anything anyone would like to say before the group ends and mention the topic of the next session (feeling good about yourself). Remind students of the confidentiality rule and the time for the next meeting.

Role Play Situations List

1. Your mom and dad are arguing about who will be allowed to come to your birthday party. You are watching them argue.

   Roles: Mom, Dad, you

2. You are watching your favorite TV show on the only set in the house when your mom brings home her new boyfriend. She asks you to go to your room or the den tonight so they can watch another show.

   Roles: Mom, boyfriend, you

3. Your teacher is fussing at your friend for not doing his/her homework. You know your friend's dad just moved out last night, but the teacher does not.

   Roles: Friend, teacher, you

4. Your mother is fuming mad because your dad has promised to send the child support check for the past 3 weeks. She just went to the mailbox and, again, the check wasn't there. She is now on the phone to your dad. You are listening in.

   Roles: Mom, Dad, you

5. Your dad's new girlfriend comes to pick you up instead of your dad. Your mother is angry and won't let you go.

   Roles: Mom, Dad's girlfriend, you

6. Your stepfather calls you "kid" and slaps you. Your mother is just walking in the door.

   Roles: Stepfather, Mom, you

Feeling Good about Myself

Goals

1. To help students learn to identify their positive characteristics and share positive things about themselves
2. To improve students' self-concept by encouraging them to accept positive feedback from others
3. To help students recognize that they are good people even if they have problems in their families

Materials

Chalkboard or chart paper

A full-length mirror with edges bound with heavy tape for safety

Process

Review

1. Ask students whether anyone noticed how other family members might be feeling about various situations or was able to tell someone they understood that person's point of view. Discuss responses.

Working Time

1. Briefly describe the goals of the session.
2. Share with students that, although many negative things may happen during a divorce, positive things also happen—for example, learning to get along with new people, sharing thoughts and feelings, and learning new skills (e.g., negotiating and expressing opinions, needs, and wants).
3. Make several columns on the chalkboard or chart paper, using headings such as *The Person I Am, Friends, Schoolwork, Hobbies/Sports,* and *Family.* (Other categories may be used as desired.) Ask students to share what they do well or like about themselves in each category. Write down responses as they are given. For example:

The Person I Am	Friends	Schoolwork	Hobbies/Sports	Family
Shawn:				
friendly, sad	has lots	likes computer stuff	good basketball player	new stepdad and stepsister
Suzanne:				
quiet, smart	would like to make more	likes art	rides in local horse shows	just Mom and me now

4. After each student has responded, point out that it is important to feel good about ourselves even if things are not going well in our families. Get out the mirror and model looking in it and saying three nice things to yourself. For example: "Well, let's see. I have a friendly face. I like the way I wear my hair. And I like being a counselor at this school."
5. Pass the mirror to a volunteer. The volunteer is to hold the mirror and say three positive things. The leader then says one positive thing about the person, then allows the other students to contribute three more. For example: "Jill, you have such a delightful smile."

6. Allow each group member to hold the mirror and experience saying and receiving positive comments, then discuss the following questions.
   - How did you feel when you were standing in front of the mirror and saying nice things about yourself?
   - Was it hard for you to believe the things other people said?
   - What did you like or dislike about doing this exercise?
   - Do you think it may be easier for you to think positively about yourself in the future? If so, why?

Closing Time

1. Invite students to practice making positive statements outside the group, both to themselves and to others.
2. Ask whether there is anything anyone would like to say before the group ends and mention the topic of the final session (reviewing what has been learned in the group and saying goodbye). Remind students of the confidentiality rule and the time for the next meeting.

Saying Goodbye

Goals

1. To provide a review of what has happened in the past seven sessions
2. To help students understand and cope with the fact that the group is ending
3. To illustrate the importance of saying goodbye and give students a chance to achieve closure on the group and their relationships in it

Materials

Construction paper in assorted colors
Marking pens in assorted colors
Two or three stamp pads

Process

Review

1. Invite students to share their experiences making positive statements to themselves and others.
2. Next, go through the session topics and discuss what students feel are the most important lessons they learned in the group. The following questions may be helpful.
   - What did you learn about the new names used to describe relationships in your family? (Session 2)
   - What did you learn from knowing about other students' living arrangements? (Session 3)
   - What did you learn about your own and others' beliefs about divorce? (Session 4)
   - What feelings did you learn to recognize in yourself? How did you learn to express them? (Session 5)
   - What did you find out about other people's feelings from role playing? (Session 6)
   - What good things did you discover about yourself or about others? (Session 7)

Working Time

1. Point out that all relationships come to an end, whether by moving away or mutual decision, or for other reasons. Encourage students to talk about their own experiences with having relationships end.
2. Discuss the importance of goodbyes, stressing that saying goodbye can help people deal with sadness when a relationship ends and go on to new relationships.
3. Pass out the art materials, explaining that students will be making "goodbye cards" to help them leave the group. Have each student fold a piece of construction paper in half. On the front, have students write their names and "says goodbye" (e.g., "Shawn says goodbye"). They then ink the fingers of one hand and press their fingerprints around these words. Group members pass their goodbye cards around so other students can sign their names and write a short message inside. (Be sure to sign each student's card yourself.)

Closing Time

1. Remind students of the confidentiality rule. Thank them for participating and tell them that, even though the group is ending, you will continue to be available to them (if this is indeed the case) and that you hope the friendships made in the group will continue.
2. Encourage students to have a "group hug" if the atmosphere seems right.

Meeting, Making, and Keeping Friends

Having friendship skills and being able to make friends successfully is very important for the young adolescent. Friends provide social reinforcement, models of behavior and values, and learning experiences in forming and ending relationships. In addition, a significant body of research indicates that deficiencies in social interaction skills can have an effect on academic achievement, as well as a lasting impact well into adulthood (e.g., Cobb & Hops, 1973; Hartup, 1976).

Young children do not have the capacity to empathize with another person, to see things from another's perspective (Selman, 1980). However, during early adolescence this pattern of social cognition changes. The young adolescent has an increased capacity to form emotional bonds, to learn the concepts of loyalty and honest communication, and to be intimate and loving (Adams & Gullotta, 1989; Steinberg, 1985). These qualities, and the ability to understand another person's point of view, are at the heart of friendships and, later on, love relationships.

Studies in the area of adolescent development have established that popular children possess friendly and cooperative attitudes, as well as the ability to communicate honestly. Those judged by their peers as less popular frequently behave in either an aggressive or extremely shy manner, exhibit inappropriate behavior, do not conform to norms of the peer group, and have poor communication skills (Hartup, 1983). Youth who have few friends and who lack communication skills are frequently lonely and unhappy.

Many of the behaviors associated with problems in developing and maintaining friendships have responded well to social skills training using cognitive-behavioral techniques and group counseling. Some of these behavioral target areas are inappropriate assertion (Barrett & Yarrow, 1977; Bornstein, Bellack, & Hersen, 1977), isolated/withdrawn behaviors (Edelson & Rose, 1981; Lew & Mesch, 1984), predelinquent and delinquent behaviors (Gross, Brigham, Hopper, & Bologna, 1980; Hazel, Schumaker, Sherman, & Sheldon-Wildgen, 1982), and learning disabilities and difficulties (LaGreca & Mesibov, 1979).

Group Objectives

1. To encourage understanding of what it means to be a friend and to have friends
2. To replace students' nonconstructive friendship behaviors with more appropriate ones
3. To help students distinguish between thoughts, feelings, and behaviors and learn to deal appropriately with negative feelings in friendship situations
4. To encourage students to seek out new friends and understand the "clique phenomenon"
5. To provide a safe, accepting environment for members to explore new skills

Selection and Other Guidelines

The following target signs may indicate that a student is a candidate for this particular group experience.

1. Passive behaviors such as poor eye contact; minimal class participation; withdrawal or shyness; submission to bullying; and lack of participation in school clubs, teams, or organizations
2. Aggressive behaviors such as fighting, bullying, name-calling, stealing, or disruptiveness in class
3. Expressions of low self-esteem—for example, achievement at a lower level than expected or limited contacts with peers

In addition to following the general selection criteria outlined in the Introduction, select students with heterogeneous abilities in social skills. A good mix would include two or three members who are shy but who want to make friends, two or three who are lacking in communication skills or are perhaps new to the school, and one or two who are abrasive in some way (perhaps bullying or hurtful). The major consideration is not to overload the group with one type, either all very shy or all very aggressive.

References and Recommended Reading

Adams, G. R., & Gullotta, T. (1989). *Adolescent life experiences.* Belmont, CA: Brooks/Cole.

Barrett, D. E., & Yarrow, M. R. (1977). Prosocial behavior, social inferential ability, and assertiveness in children. *Child Development, 48,* 475–481.

Bornstein, M. R., Bellack, A. S., & Hersen, M. (1977). Social-skills training for unassertive children: A multiple-baseline analysis. *Journal of Applied Behavior Analysis, 10,* 183–195.

Cobb, J. A., & Hops, H. (1973). Effects of academic survival skills training on low achieving first graders. *The Journal of Educational Research, 67,* 108–113.

Conger, J. C., & Keane, S. P. (1981). Social skills intervention in the treatment of isolated or withdrawn children. *Psychological Bulletin, 90,* 478–493.

Edelson, J. L., & Rose, S. D. (1981). Investigations into the efficacy of short-term group social skills training for socially isolated children. *Child Behavior Therapy, 3,* 1-16.

Goldstein, A. P., Sprafkin, R. P., Gershaw, N. J., & Klein, P. (1980). *Skillstreaming the adolescent: A structured learning approach to teaching prosocial skills.* Champaign, IL: Research Press.

Gross, A., Brigham, T. A., Hopper, C., & Bologna, N. (1980). Self-management and social skills training: A study with predelinquent and delinquent youths. *Criminal Justice and Behavior, 7,* 161–184.

Hartup, W. W. (1970). Peer interaction and social organization. In P. H. Mussen (Ed.), *Carmichael's manual of child psychology* (Vol. 2, 3rd ed.). New York: Wiley.

Hartup, W. W. (1976). Peer interaction and the behavioral development of the individual child. In E. Schopler & R. Reichler (Eds.), *Psychopathology and child development.* New York: Plenum.

Hartup, W. W. (1983). The peer system. In P. H. Mussen (Ed.), *Carmichael's manual of child psychology* (Vol. 4, 4th ed.). New York: Wiley.

Hazel, J. S., Schumaker, J. B., Sherman, J. A., & Sheldon-Wildgen, J. (1982). Group training for social skills: A program for court adjudicated, probationary youths. *Criminal Justice and Behavior, 9,* 35–53.

LaGreca, A. M., & Mesibov, G. B. (1979). Social skills intervention with learning disabled children: Selecting skills and implementing training. *Journal of Clinical Child Psychology, 8,* 234–241.

Lew, M., & Mesch, D. (1984, August). *Isolated students in secondary schools: Cooperative group contingencies and social skills training.* Paper presented at the annual convention of the American Psychological Association, Toronto.

Selman, R. L. (1980). *The growth of interpersonal understanding.* New York: Academic.

Steinberg, L. (1985). *Adolescence.* New York: Knopf.

Walker, H. M., & Hops, H. (1976). Increasing academic achievement by reinforcing direct academic performance and/or facilitative nonacademic responses. *Journal of Educational Psychology, 68,* 218–225.

Getting Started

Goals

1. To help students become acquainted and begin to feel comfortable in the group setting
2. To choose appropriate ground rules for the group sessions
3. To identify why students want to be a part of the group and what they hope to learn

Materials

Sample Record of Me
Record of Me Form
Chalkboard or chart paper

Process

Ice Breaker

1. Welcome students and briefly describe the goals of the group in general as well as this session in particular.
2. Propose the idea that, when a songwriter composes a song, that person wants to share his or her ideas with others. Tell students they also will be undertaking a brief activity to share some things about themselves.
3. Distribute one copy of the Record of Me Form to each student. Instruct students to choose six categories from the following list and create a Record of Me like the sample provided. (One of the categories must be *What I Hope to Accomplish in Group.*)
   - My Favorite Song
   - My Favorite Place to Go with Friends
   - My Best Friend
   - Month of Birth
   - My Pet(s)
   - Best Vacation Ever
   - Class I Like Best
   - Sport I Like/Do Best
   - Favorite Movie
   - Favorite Performing Artist
   - Favorite Food
   - Where I Was Born
   - Best Friend in Elementary School
   - Favorite Restaurant
   - What I Hope to Accomplish in Group
4. Give students about 5 minutes to work, then ask them to pair up with the person next to them and share the information they have selected about themselves.
5. Ask students to take turns introducing their partners and telling what they have learned. For example: "Lisa shared her record, and she likes pizza better than anything else in the world! She was born in April, has a cat named Tigger, and her best vacation ever was skiing in Colorado. She loves Bruce Springsteen and is in the group because she wants to learn ways to meet a boyfriend."

Sample Record of Me

Working Time

1. Introduce the idea of ground rules, pointing out that rules help everyone be respected and have time to talk. Suggest a few basic ground rules, such as the following.
   - What we say and do here is private and stays in the group (confidentiality rule).
   - Everyone has the right to "pass"—that is, not to participate in an activity or part of an activity.
   - No fighting or arguing.
   - Each person gets time to talk.
   - When someone is talking, everyone else will listen.
2. Ask students to think of other ground rules for the group. List all rules on the chalkboard or on chart paper.

Closing Time

1. Share some positive observations about the session. For example: "Ray, I appreciate your helping us understand what will be expected in the group"; "I really liked how you shared your idea about friendship, Shawn"; or "Teri, I'm glad you have decided to be a part of the group."
2. Ask whether there is anything anyone would like to say before the group ends and mention the topic of the next session (finding out what it means to be a friend). Remind students of the confidentiality rule and the time for the next meeting.

Record of Me Form

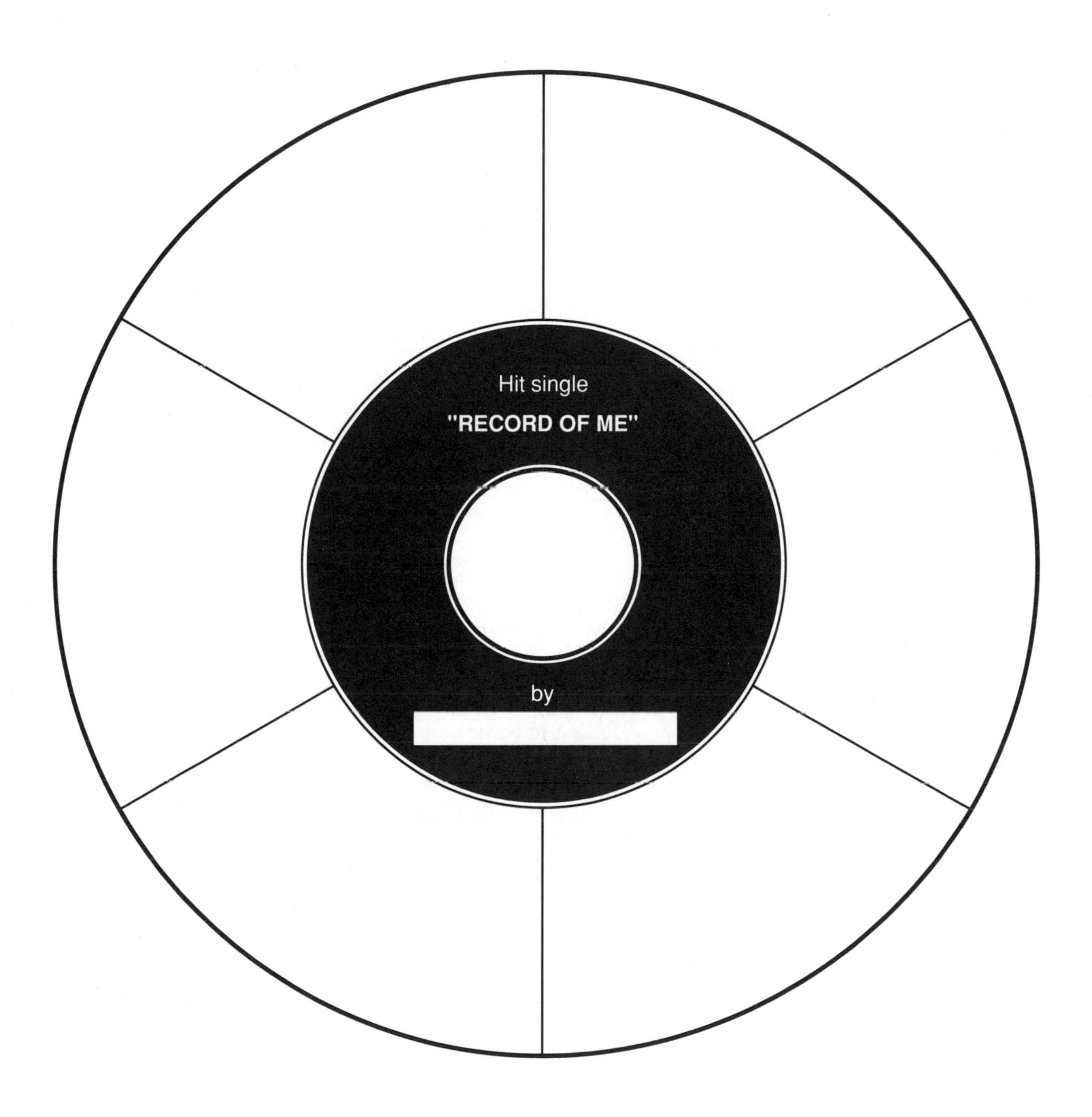

What Does It Mean to Be a Friend?

Goals

1. To allow students to define friendship in their own terms
2. To illustrate the major components of friendship
3. To suggest how students can make new friends and become closer to the friends they have

Materials

Roll paper (approximately 3 × 6 feet)
Marking pens in assorted colors
Sample Session 2 Behavior Record
Session 2 Behavior Record

Process

Review

1. Invite students to recall as much information from Session 1 as they can about other group members.

Working Time

1. Briefly describe the goals of the session.
2. Ask for two volunteers: One person lies down on the piece of roll paper, and the other traces around that person's body with a marking pen to make a "person outline." Have two more volunteers turn the paper over and do the same on the reverse side.
3. Invite students to think of the qualities they value in a friend. These might include honesty, loyalty, willingness to be there for you, friendliness, affection, helpfulness, and so forth. As students make suggestions, have them come up and write the values somewhere on the front side of the person outline. Allow each student to contribute two or more values.
4. Stimulate a discussion among students of the values they selected. For example: "Jill, you mentioned that you value 'being friendly.' Would you explain what that means to you?"; "Teri, you and Tom both said friends are always honest. What would it be like for you if a friend lied to you?"; or "Pat mentioned that best friends never get mad at each other. What does it mean when you get mad at a friend?"
5. Turn the person outline over and invite students to identify qualities they do not value in a friend. These might include lying, tattling, backbiting, fighting, name-calling, bullying, and so forth. Allow students to write two or more of these types of behaviors on the back side of the person outline.
6. Point out that to be a friend and have friends we need to show lots of the qualities listed on the front side of the person outline and avoid doing the things listed on the back side.

Closing Time

1. Pass out copies of the Session 2 Behavior Record, explaining that, if we are serious about replacing negative behaviors with positive ones, we first need to find out exactly what needs to be changed. Using the Sample Session 2 Behavior Record to illustrate, instruct students to watch for positive and negative friendship behaviors and to write down situations when these occur.
2. Ask whether there is anything anyone would like to say before the group ends and mention the topic of the next session (changing friendship behaviors). Remind students of the confidentiality rule and the time for the next meeting.

Name *Bill S.* Date *3/5/90*

Sample Session 2 Behavior Record

Instructions: Write down situations in which you see positive or negative friendship behaviors. Then write down what you think and feel in each situation.

Day	What Happened	What I Think/Feel
Monday	*My brother hit his friend, Shawn. Shawn went home crying.*	*Hitting people makes them angry and hurt.*
Tuesday	*My brother helped my mom take out all the garbage.*	*Helping people makes them feel nice.*
Wednesday	*The teacher called a kid stupid.*	*Calling names hurts. I don't like it when adults do this.*
Thursday	*I shoved a guy in the lunch line, and he knocked me down.*	*I guess I shouldn't butt in, but waiting my turn takes longer!*
Friday	*I saw a girl crying, and I said, "It's OK."*	*She smiled, and I felt good.*

Name____ Date____________________

Session 2 Behavior Record

Instructions: Write down situations in which you see positive or negative friendship behaviors. Then write down what you think and feel in each situation.

Day	What Happened	What I Think/Feel

Changing Friendship Behaviors

Goals

1. To help students discover what they and others like and don't like about them
2. To provide a way for students to decrease negative friendship behaviors and increase positive ones

Materials

Session 2 Behavior Record (self-improvement exercise from Session 2)
Sample Session 3 Behavior Record
Session 3 Behavior Record

Process

Review

1. Invite students to share information from their Session 2 Behavior Records about situations in which they saw positive or negative friendship behaviors. Give students a chance to describe the situations they wrote down and tell what they learned from observing friendship behaviors.

Working Time

1. Briefly describe the goals of the session.
2. Ask students what kinds of things they themselves could begin doing (or stop doing) that might make them a better friend. Stress that they should think of things they do that are positive or attractive to others and things they do that may be negative or turn-offs to others. Model self-disclosure by sharing some of your own positive and negative qualities. For example: "My positive friendship behaviors are that I smile and say 'Good morning' to nearly everyone I meet when I get to work each day, and I think that makes people begin conversations with me. I look people in the eye when I talk to them, and people also know they can depend on me to be there if they need to talk. A negative behavior I need to work on is having a grumpy attitude when I get up in the morning. It makes me unpleasant to be around, and I don't like treating my family this way."
3. Have students pair up. Ask each partner to share three positive behaviors and one negative behavior, as you have just done. Positive behaviors might include being cooperative, having an upbeat attitude, knowing how to start a conversation, being a good listener, being able to stand up for your own ideas, being able to give compliments, and so forth. Negative behaviors might include being moody, not being able to apologize when you are wrong, getting into fights, being disloyal, acting as though you feel unworthy of having friends, and so forth.
4. Invite students to share with the group at least one positive and one negative friendship behavior. Because disclosing something negative about oneself can be threatening, strongly praise those who go first and don't insist that everyone participate.
5. Point out that we are not born knowing how to make and keep friends; rather, we have learned to be the way we are. That means we can change how we are by learning new ways to do things. In order to determine whether or not we are successful in reducing negative friendship behaviors and increasing positive ones, we need to keep track of our *target behaviors*. For example, if you want to stop being grouchy in the morning, you might choose making positive comments instead as your target behavior.

Closing Time

1. Distribute copies of the Session 3 Behavior Record. Ask each student to identify a friendship target behavior to work on. (Students may need some individual help in choosing a manageable target behavior and defining it clearly.) Use the Sample Session 3 Behavior Record to illustrate the types of entries students are expected to make.
2. Ask whether there is anything anyone would like to say before the group ends and mention the topic of the next session (learning introduction and conversation skills). Remind students of the confidentiality rule and the time for the next meeting.

Name *Ms. Bennie* Date *3/12/90*

Sample Session 3 Behavior Record

Instructions: Write your target behavior in the space below, then keep track of your progress.

Target Behavior: *Having a pleasant facial expression and saying something pleasant to each family member in the morning (not being crabby or grouchy).*

Day	What Happened	What I Think/Feel
Monday	*Got up late, everything behind schedule, fussed at three people.*	*Felt down because I yelled instead of asking nicely. I know they were upset with me.*
Tuesday	*Did not say positive statements I had planned to.*	*Wish I had been more positive but am pleased I didn't gripe.*
Wednesday	*Smiled and said, "Good morning" to each family member. Did not fuss at anyone.*	*Felt much better than yesterday!*
Thursday	*Felt like complaining at breakfast but didn't.*	*Felt like I had done a good job.*
Friday	*Got up early and said one nice statement to each family member.*	*Pleased that I was not negative in the morning.*

Name____ Date________________

Session 3 Behavior Record

Instructions: Write your target behavior in the space below, then keep track of your progress.

Target Behavior:

Day	What Happened	What I Think/Feel

Introduction and Conversation Skills

Goals

1. To illustrate introduction skills and to provide practice in making introductions
2. To show students how to start conversations and to provide practice in conversation skills

Materials

Session 3 Behavior Record (self-improvement exercise from Session 3)
Sample Session 4 Behavior Record
Session 4 Behavior Record

Process

Review

1. Discuss what results students obtained from their assignment last session to work on a friendship target behavior. Invite them to share the responses they made on the Session 3 Behavior Record. Discuss the following questions.
   - Were you successful in reaching your target goal in terms of increasing a positive friendship behavior?
   - Did you catch yourself before doing something negative?
   - What did it feel like when you did something positive instead of your old, negative behavior?

Working Time

1. Briefly discuss the goals of the session.
2. Point out that, if you don't know how to make introductions or begin conversations, a friendship may never start. Sometimes we feel as though we'd like to know someone, but we just don't know how to begin. The following steps are helpful.
   - Approach the person you want to meet.
   - Say "Hello," "Hi," or give some other greeting.
   - Say "My name is ________________________________."
   - Wait for the person to say his or her name or say, "What's your name?"

   All together, the steps sound like this: "Hi, my name's Jill. What's your name?"
3. Model these steps by having students introduce themselves to you.
4. After all students have practiced introducing themselves, describe how to introduce two people to each other.
   - Look at the first person and say that person's name.
   - Tell the first person the second person's name.
   - Repeat the process with the second person.

   All together, the steps sound like this: "Jill, this is Teri Homes. Teri, this is Jill Bonney."
5. Have students form groups of three and practice introducing one another.
6. After all students have had a chance to make a two-person introduction, point out that a conversation frequently follows an introduction. The following steps are involved in starting a conversation.
   - Look at the person with whom you want to speak.
   - Say something about yourself (for example, something you like).

- Ask the person about something he or she likes.
- Make a positive comment about what the person said.

All together, the steps sound like this: "I like playing football and track. What kind of sports do you like? (*Response:* I like track too, but I don't know much about it.) You can come to our practice tonight if you like." Or, "I enjoy working on the computer a lot. What do you like best at school? (*Response:* I like to go to the library and check out magazines.) Oh, sometimes I get *People Magazine* at the store. I like reading about celebrities."

7. Have students pair up and practice starting conversations.
8. After students have practiced starting conversations, discuss the following questions.
   - What is it like for you to be introduced?
   - What is it like to be the person making an introduction, either of yourself or another person?
   - What kinds of feelings do you have when you start a conversation with someone new?
   - What would you do if a person didn't want to keep talking with you?

Closing Time

1. Ask students whether they think they could use these skills sometime before the next session. Distribute copies of the Session 4 Behavior Record and negotiate how many introductions and conversations the group feel they could practice (three introductions and three conversations would be a good number). Use the Sample Session 4 Behavior Record to illustrate the types of entries students are expected to make.
2. Ask whether there is anything anyone would like to say before the group ends and mention the topic of the next session (recognizing the difference between thoughts, feelings, and behaviors). Remind students of the confidentiality rule and the time for the next meeting.

Name *Trent A.* Date *3/19/90*

Sample Session 4 Behavior Record

Instructions: Write down the times you practiced making an introduction or starting a conversation.

Day	Introduction/Conversation	What I Think/Feel
Monday	*I said, "Hi, my name is Keith. I play guard. What position do you play?"*	*I was so scared my knees shook.*
Tuesday	*I said, "You look nice, Cheryl."*	*I was afraid she wouldn't answer me, but she said "Thanks."*
Wednesday	*I wanted to say something to Caitlin, but I didn't.*	*I like her a lot, but I just couldn't get up the nerve.*
Thursday	*I told Tyler to leave my sister alone.*	*I was glad I said it!*
Friday	*I asked Caitlin if she was going to the game tonight and if she would sit with me.*	*I felt good that she said yes.*

Name________________________________ Date______________

Session 4 Behavior Record

Instructions: Write down the times you practiced making an introduction or starting a conversation.

Day	Introduction/Conversation	What I Think/Feel

Thoughts, Feelings, and Behaviors

Goals

1. To introduce the idea that negative feelings may cause friendships to end
2. To help students differentiate between feelings, thoughts, and behaviors and to recognize their feelings outside of the group situation
3. To prepare students for Session 6 (Processing Negative Feelings)

Materials

Session 4 Behavior Record (self-improvement exercise from Session 4)
Index cards (labeled with thought, feeling, or behavior words)
Feelings Chart (from the group *Dealing with a Divorce in the Family,* p. 24)
Chalkboard or chart paper

Process

Review

1. Ask students to report on their experiences meeting new people or starting conversations, as noted on their Session 4 Behavior Records. The following discussion questions may be helpful.
    - What pleasant things came from your practicing introductions?
    - Were there any unpleasant outcomes?
    - How do you think being able to make introductions or start conversations will help you in the future?

Working Time

1. Briefly describe the goals of the session.
2. Discuss what sorts of things happen to cause people to end friendships. Examples might include lack of communication, finding out the other person has very different values or incompatible behaviors, dishonesty, problems due to time or distance, and negative feelings.
3. Point out that negative feelings like anger, fear, or jealousy often cause friendships to break up but that these feelings are as much a part of us as more positive feelings like love, affection, and joy. Ask students to share some of the negative feelings they may have had in friendship situations. Explain that Session 6 will present a way of dealing with negative feelings but that to use this method, students must first understand the difference between thoughts, feelings, and behaviors.
4. Distribute two or three index cards to each student. (Prepare these cards in advance by labeling them with various thought, feeling, and behavior words, as shown.) Explain that thoughts are processes that take place in the brain, feelings are expressions of emotion, and behaviors are things we do.

Thoughts	Feelings	Behaviors
remember	joy	running
idea	anger	watching TV
think	fear	kissing
figure	depression	discussing
forget	delight	arguing
ponder	worry	working
cogitate	loneliness	doing dishes

5. Give a few examples of thoughts, feelings, or behaviors and ask the group as a whole to guess the different categories to which the examples belong. Then have each student read his or her card aloud and identify the appropriate category. Continue until students appear to have grasped the concept.

Closing Time

1. Distribute one copy of the Feelings Chart to each student and explain that the chart contains many words to express each of the emotions listed. In addition, the words are grouped by level of intensity (e.g., if you are extremely happy, you might be *radiant;* if very happy, *tickled;* if mildly happy, *glad*). Ask students whether they would be willing to pay attention to what feelings they experience in friendship situations. Instruct them to put a checkmark in front of any feelings they experience between this time and the next session. If a particular feeling is not represented on the list, students may write it on the back of the page. Stress that the reason you are asking students to use the Feelings Chart is so that they become aware of the intense feelings friendships produce.
2. Ask whether there is anything anyone would like to say before the group ends and mention the topic of the next session (processing negative feelings). Remind students of the confidentiality rule and the time for the next meeting.

Processing Negative Feelings

Goals

1. To provide practice in expressing negative emotions relating to friendships
2. To help students learn the skill of using *I messages* when experiencing strong feelings or needs

Materials

Feelings Chart (self-improvement exercise from Session 5)
Sample Session 6 Behavior Record
Session 6 Behavior Record

Process

Review

1. Invite students to share some of the feelings they experienced since the last session. Encourage them to use their completed Feelings Charts in the discussion and to answer the question "What was it like for you when you felt . . . "

Working Time

1. Briefly describe the goals of the session.
2. Review some of the negative feelings students mentioned in Session 5 as being associated with friendships and ask them to explain what they did when they had these feelings. Responses may range from "I just don't go around that person anymore" (possibly nonassertive behavior) to "We have big fights" (possibly aggressive behavior) to "I just keep to myself" (possibly depressive behavior). Explain that such responses may be successful in dealing with negative feelings in the short run but that none of these really resolves the problem.
3. Introduce the idea that the best way of dealing with negative feelings is to *process* them, or express them honestly to the person or people involved. Stress that the way to do this is to use *I messages* as opposed to *you messages.* To illustrate, provide several examples of *you messages.*
   - You are a turkey for not lending me your homework so I can copy it.
   - You are stupid.
   - You should have done your work.
   - Why didn't you do it right?
4. Discuss how *you messages* make students feel (accused, put down, hurt, angry, turned off, blamed, etc.). Point out that *you messages* hurt when they are received.
5. Help students contrast *you messages* with *I messages,* which allow people to state their feelings without hurting someone else. Present the following two formulas for *I messages.*

   I feel __________ because __________, and I'd like __________.

   I feel __________ when __________, and I needed to tell you that.

6. Elicit several feelings the group might like to share and fit them into these formulas. For example:
   - Sharin says she hates it when her friends don't ask her to go along to the mall. She could say, "I feel *left out* when *you go to the mall without me,* and I needed to tell you that."
   - Juan says he feels angry when Marty breaks his pens. He could say, "I feel *angry when you break my pens* because *I don't have money to blow,* and I'd like *you to quit it.*"

7. Ask for a volunteer to practice using *I messages* to handle a negative feeling and another volunteer who will listen and react to the first volunteer's statement. Place two chairs facing each other in the center of the group and have the volunteers sit as they role play the situation. Following the role play, ask the following discussion questions.

   To the first volunteer

   - What was it like for you to use this kind of message?
   - Would you be willing to try this outside the group?

   To the second volunteer

   - What kinds of thoughts and feelings did you experience when you received the *I message?*
   - In what ways might the message make you feel uncomfortable?

8. Allow as many students to practice role plays as time allows. Encourage those who are not participating directly to observe and comment on each role play.

Closing Time

1. Discuss with students whether they would be willing to practice using *I messages* three times before the group meets again. Distribute copies of the Session 6 Behavior Record and instruct students to record their experiences. Use the Sample Session 6 Behavior Record to illustrate the type of responses students are expected to make.
2. Ask whether there is anything anyone else would like to say before the group ends and mention the topic of the next session (making more friends). Remind students of the confidentiality rule and the time for the next meeting.

Name *Beth R.* Date *4/7/90*

Sample Session 6 Behavior Record

Instructions: Write down your experiences in practicing *I messages.*

Day	I Message	What I Think/Feel
Monday	*I get mad when the Coke is all gone when I get home from the game hot and tired.*	*I'm glad I said it. Maybe she'll replace the empty bottle with a full one.*
Tuesday	*Dad, I get upset when Stevie gets more allowance than I do.*	*Maybe Dad will see my side now and give me more!*
Wednesday	*I feel accused when you say, "Sure, you don't smoke."*	*I'm glad I said it because I've been feeling this way a long time.*
Thursday	*When my clothes are borrowed without my being asked, I feel angry.*	*Stop taking my clothes without my permission!*
Friday	*I feel overloaded with so much homework.*	*I think Mr. Thomas shouldn't give us so much homework on weekends.*

Name____ Date____________________

Session 6 Behavior Record

Instructions: Write down your experiences in practicing *I messages.*

Day	I Message	What I Think/Feel

Making More Friends

Goals

1. To use brainstorming as a technique to help students discover new ways to make friends
2. To help students understand the effects of cliques and decide whether or not they want to belong to certain groups
3. To encourage students to avoid making other people feel left out

Materials

Session 6 Behavior Record (self-improvement exercise from Session 6)
Chalkboard or chart paper

Process

Review

1. Invite students to share their experiences using *I messages,* as recorded on their Session 6 Behavior Records. The following discussion questions may be helpful.
   - What happened when you used an *I message?*
   - How did the other person react?
   - What did you think and feel after you made the statement?

Working Time

1. Briefly describe the goals of the session.
2. Instruct students to form two teams to brainstorm as many ways as they can to make new friends. After 10–15 minutes, have teams reconvene. Encourage teams to share their ideas by writing them on the chalkboard or chart paper. Some possible suggestions are as follows.
   - Sit beside someone different in the cafeteria and say "Hi."
   - Offer to show someone new in the school around the building.
   - Join a club or the band.
   - Offer to help someone carry a heavy load.
   - Ask someone you know to introduce you to new people.
   - Go to the gym or track after school and say hello to the kids practicing.
   - Start talking to someone who has an interesting library book.
3. Help students define the term *clique* in their own words (an in-group or gang of popular kids). Discuss the difficulties cliques cause in making new friends, stressing that the reason many kids want to be part of a clique is that they want to be liked by important people and feel important themselves.
4. Discuss the following questions, encouraging students to explore whether or not they want to belong to certain groups and to define criteria they could use to decide whether the group is good for them or not. (The idea of one's "reputation" is likely to come up in this context.)
   - In what ways do you think cliques are good?
   - In what ways do you think cliques are harmful?
   - What does it mean for you to belong to a clique?
   - What would happen if there were no cliques at this school?
   - Are there cliques after you get out of school?
   - Do adults have cliques?

Closing Time

1. Ask students whether they would be willing to try to make one new friend before the next session and to do something they like with the friend, such as sit next to each other at a pep rally, eat lunch together, or play video games after school. Also ask them to pay particular attention to the "clique phenomenon" and make an effort to avoid trying to make other people feel left out.
2. Ask whether there is anything anyone would like to say before the group ends and mention the topic of the final session (reviewing what has been learned in the group and saying goodbye). Remind students of the confidentiality rule and the time for the next meeting.

Saying Goodbye

Goals

1. To provide a review of what has happened in the past seven sessions
2. To help students realize that friendships end and cope with the fact that the group is ending
3. To illustrate the importance of saying goodbye and give students a chance to achieve closure on the group and their relationships in it

Materials

Paper lunch bags

Strips of paper (approximately 2 × 8 inches each)

Marking pens in assorted colors

Process

Review

1. Invite students to share their experiences in meeting new friends and in noticing cliques.
2. Next, go through the session topics and discuss what students feel are the most important lessons they learned in the group. The following questions may be helpful.
    - What did you learn about what qualities you do and don't value in friendships? (Session 2)
    - What positive and negative friendship behaviors did you learn about? How can you change your negative behaviors into positive ones? (Session 3)
    - How did you learn to introduce yourself to others and begin conversations? (Session 4)
    - What is the difference between thoughts, feelings, and behaviors, and why is it important to be able to tell one from the other? (Session 5)
    - How did you learn to deal with negative feelings in friendships? (Session 6)
    - What are some of the ways you can make new friends? How can you decide whether or not it is good to belong to a clique? (Session 7)

Working Time

1. Point out that during the past sessions the group has shared much information and some very personal feelings about friends and friendship. Explain that this session will involve an exercise to help students leave the group with positive feelings about themselves and other group members.
2. Give each student a paper lunch sack and a blank strip of paper for each other group member, including yourself. Instruct students to write their own names on the sack and the names of the other group members on the separate strips of paper. Then have the students write on the various strips of paper one positive comment about each person in the group (e.g., something nice that person did or something special he or she contributed). Distribute your own positive comments (which you have prepared in advance) to get the students started. Give students 10–15 minutes to complete this task and to distribute their strips to other group members. Explain that these "good feelings" are to take away with them and that they should not look at them until later.
3. When students have finished, discuss how all friendships come to an end, whether by moving away or mutual decision, or for other reasons. Encourage students to talk about their own experiences with having friendships end.
4. Discuss the importance of goodbyes, stressing that saying goodbye can help people deal with sadness when a friendship ends and go on to meet new friends.

5. Model saying goodbye to each student, expressing one thing you will miss about that person. For example: "Goodbye, Marty! I'll miss your special way of making us laugh at ourselves." Encourage students to say goodbye to one another in the same fashion.

Closing Time

1. Remind students of the confidentiality rule. Thank them for participating and tell them that, even though the group is ending, you will continue to be available to them (if this is indeed the case) and that you hope the friendships made in the group will continue.
2. Encourage students to have a "group hug" if the atmosphere seems right.

Communicate Straight: Learning Assertion Skills

Young adolescents frequently lack the skills to share their wants, needs, ideas, and feelings accurately and responsibly. Some behave nonassertively, perhaps because they are reinforced for passive behavior or because they simply lack the knowledge and skills to assert themselves. Others behave aggressively, perhaps because aggression is effective in getting them what they want or because it is the only way they know how to survive in their environment. Either approach can result in negative feelings: worthlessness, guilt, anger at self and others, and powerlessness (Jakubowski & Lange, 1978). Learning the difference between nonassertive, assertive, and aggressive behavior and mastering the skills associated with being appropriately assertive are ways youngsters can improve their self-expression and increase personal responsibility for behavior (Alberti & Emmons, 1986; Galassi & Galassi, 1977).

Being able to respond assertively is especially important for students at this developmental point. In terms of acquiring interpersonal relationship skills, students are learning to be more independent in general but are at the same time frequently insecure about their relationships with peers and dependent on peer approval and companionship (Adams & Gullotta, 1989). Without assertion skills, students may be unable to resist peer pressure and may experience a loss of self-esteem. In addition, their maladaptive ways of relating to others may stay with them for years and become quite resistant to change.

Research has shown that assertion skills can be taught, practiced, and generalized to other situations (Lange & Jakubowski, 1976). As such, this group counseling experience can be an important stimulus to youngsters' social development.

Group Objectives

1. To help students discriminate among nonassertive, assertive, and aggressive communication styles
2. To communicate the idea that people have certain personal rights and that these rights form the basis for assertive behavior
3. To provide opportunities to discuss and practice assertion skills so students can actively choose the way they behave
4. To help students recognize positive assertions, personal rights assertions, and negative assertions, and to give students practice in making these assertions
5. To encourage students to use assertion skills in appropriate situations outside the group

Selection and Other Guidelines

The following target signs may indicate that a student is a candidate for this particular group experience.

1. Extreme shyness resulting in the student's having few or no friends
2. The inability to seek simple information or request that basic needs be met
3. A pattern of letting other students take advantage, then becoming angry
4. Angry or hostile behavior for no apparent reason
5. Overreacting to situations or the inability to control angry responses
6. Bullying or threatening behavior with peers or others

In addition to following the general selection criteria outlined in the Introduction, choose students with heterogeneous abilities in assertion skills. A good mix would include two or three members who are very nonassertive with their peers, two or three who are fairly assertive but who are lacking in communication skills or are perhaps new to the school, and one or two who are aggressive with their peers. The major consideration is not to overload the group with one type, either all very nonassertive or all very aggressive.

References and Recommended Reading

Adams, G. R., & Gullotta, T. (1989). *Adolescent life experiences.* Belmont, CA: Brooks/Cole.

Alberti, R. E., & Emmons, M. L. (1986). *Your perfect right* (5th ed. rev.). San Luis Obispo, CA: Impact.

Elgin, S. H. (1980). *The gentle art of saying no: Principles of assertiveness* (Filmstrip Kit). Pleasantville, NY: Sunburst Communications.

Galassi, M. D., & Galassi, J. P. (1977). *Assert yourself: How to be your own person.* New York: Human Sciences.

Goldstein, A. P., & Glick, B. (1987). *Aggression replacement training: A comprehensive intervention for aggressive youth.* Champaign, IL: Research Press.

Jakubowski, P., & Lange, A. J. (1978). *The assertive option: Your rights and responsibilities.* Champaign, IL: Research Press.

Lange, A. J., & Jakubowski, P. (1976). *Responsible assertive behavior: Cognitive/behavioral procedures for trainers.* Champaign, IL: Research Press.

Lloyd, S. (1988). *Developing positive assertiveness.* Los Altos, CA: Crisp.

Palmer, P. (1977). *The mouse, the monster, and me: Assertiveness for young people.* San Luis Obispo, CA: Impact.

Getting Started

Goals

1. To help students become acquainted and feel comfortable in the group setting
2. To choose appropriate ground rules for the group sessions
3. To identify why students want to be a part of the group and what they hope to learn
4. To illustrate the three major ways of interacting with others: nonassertion, aggression, and assertion

Materials

3 × 5 inch slips of construction paper in assorted colors

Marking pens in assorted colors

Straight pins

Chalkboard or chart paper

Communicate Straight Chart (prepared before the session begins and made available during all subsequent sessions)

Nonassertion, Aggression, and Assertion Worksheet

Process

Ice Breaker

1. Welcome students and briefly describe the goals of the group in general as well as this session in particular.
2. Distribute art materials and give group members a minute or so to make name tags. When tags are complete, instruct students to pin them on.
3. Ask students to pair up and share the following information: name, favorite after-school activity, and reasons for attending the group.
4. After about 5 minutes, stop the students and model the activity. For example: "My name is Ms. Suzanne Oates. I like to walk my dachshund puppy down by the river. My reason for being part of this group counseling experience is to share ways of communicating so you can get along better with other people."
5. Continue the activity by having students introduce their partners and convey the information they learned about their partners' favorite activities and reasons for coming to group.

Working Time

1. Introduce the idea of ground rules, pointing out that rules help everyone be respected and have time to talk. Suggest a few basic ground rules, such as the following.
   - What we say and do here is private and stays in the group (confidentiality rule).
   - Everyone has the right to "pass"—that is, not to participate in an activity or part of an activity.
   - No fighting or arguing.
   - Each person gets time to talk.
   - When someone is talking, everyone else will listen.
2. Ask students to think of other ground rules for the group. List all rules on the chalkboard or on chart paper.
3. Describe a problem situation that commonly occurs with young adolescents—for example, getting called an unkind name, being given a bad grade, being taken advantage of, or being asked to do something you don't want to do. Ask whether anything like this has ever happened to anyone in the group and, if so, what that person did about it. Let students share several ways they responded, such as "did nothing," "beat the kid up," "got mad but kept quiet," "didn't ask for help," or "went along with the group but didn't want to."

4. Referring to the Communicate Straight Chart, point out that we have three ways of behaving in any situation.
   - Being *nonassertive* means you don't respect your own right to express your ideas, needs, wants, feelings, and opinions. If you are nonassertive, you might be able to avoid a conflict in the short term, but, since no one knows how you feel, you probably won't get what you want or need. In addition, you may begin to feel as though no one respects you or get angry with other people for taking advantage of you.
   - Being *aggressive* means saying what you feel in a way that disregards another person's right to be respected. If you are aggressive, you may get what you want because others are afraid not to give it to you, but you may also wind up turning people off or feeling guilty for acting that way.
   - Being *assertive* means that you honestly state your feelings without denying your own right to express yourself (nonassertion) or denying the rights of others to be respected (aggression). If you are assertive, you let people know what you think, so you have a good chance of getting what you want and need. In addition, you avoid feelings of resentment, anger, and guilt, and, because you show respect for other people, you don't wind up turning them off.
5. Distribute copies of the Nonassertion, Aggression, and Assertion Worksheet and answer the questions as a group. Help students rephrase nonassertive and aggressive responses as assertive statements.

Closing Time

1. Thank students for coming to the group and praise them for their participation so far. Invite group members to pay attention during the next week to how they and other people communicate. Is their communication nonassertive, aggressive, or assertive?
2. Ask whether there is anything anyone would like to say before the group ends and mention the topic of the next session (identifying our personal rights). Remind students of the confidentiality rule and the time for the next session.

Answer Key

Nonassertion, Aggression, and Assertion Worksheet

1. AGG

   Assertive: "Your notebook really bothers me."
2. AST
3. AST
4. NON

   Assertive: "Would you get me a Pepsi, please?"
5. AGG

   Assertive: "Would you please be quiet?"
6. AST
7. NON

   Assertive: "I worked hard on this, and I don't want to share it."
8. AST
9. NON

   Assertive: "No, you can't have my money."
10. AST

Communicate Straight Chart

Being nonassertive means

Avoiding saying what you think, feel, want, or believe—

- Because you are afraid to risk the consequences
- Because you don't believe in your own rights
- Because you don't know how to speak up for yourself
- Because you think another person's rights are more important than yours

Being aggressive means

Saying what you think, feel, want, or believe—

- In ways that deny another person's right to be treated with respect (anger, meanness, hurtfulness, put-downs, spitefulness, etc.)

Being assertive means

Saying what you think, feel, want, or believe—

- In ways that don't damage another person's right to be treated with respect
- In straightforward, nonthreatening ways
- In ways that don't deny your own rights

Name____ Date____________________

Nonassertion, Aggression, and Assertion Worksheet

Instructions: Label the following statements *nonassertive* (NON), *aggressive* (AGG), or *assertive* (AST).

________ 1. I hate your stupid notebook!

________ 2. I'd really like to go to a show on Saturday.

________ 3. Would you please put your dirty clothes in the hamper after you take a bath?

________ 4. Could you possibly, I mean, maybe, get me a Pepsi? Oh well, you probably don't want to—that's OK.

________ 5. Shut up, stupid.

________ 6. I need 5 dollars for the class trip today.

________ 7. I worked really hard on this homework, but I guess I could let you copy it.

________ 8. I want you to pay me the babysitting money you owe me.

________ 9. Sure. You can have all my lunch money. No problem.

________ 10. I'm hurt that I wasn't invited to the party.

My Rights as a Person

Goals

1. To illustrate that everyone has certain rights and to help students understand appropriate ways to make their rights known
2. To encourage awareness that rights form the basis for choosing whether to be nonassertive, aggressive, or assertive

Materials

Personal Rights Handout

Process

Review

1. Ask students what they observed about their own and other people's behaviors. The following discussion questions may be helpful.
   - Was it easy or difficult to tell whether someone was communicating nonassertively, aggressively, or assertively?
   - Did you notice other people communicating in one of these three ways? What were the outcomes in these situations? How do you think these people were feeling?
   - Did you notice a time when you were using one of the three kinds of communication? What was the outcome? How did you feel?
2. Thank students for talking about their experiences and praise those who shared. For example: "Betsy, it takes real courage to tell about something you aren't proud of. I believe you are going to have a good experience in changing some of the behaviors that are causing you problems."

Working Time

1. Briefly describe the goals of the session.
2. Discuss the idea that people have certain rights just because they are human beings, then distribute copies of the Personal Rights Handout. Go around the circle, asking each group member to read one example aloud. Alternatively, ask for volunteers to read aloud any of the rights with which they particularly agree.
3. Ask students which of the rights they did not know they had. Allow time for discussion.
4. Ask students what rights they think are involved in the following situations and how they might handle them.
   - Your friend is nagging you to go to a horror movie you don't want to see and insists that if you are a true friend, you will go. You don't like horror movies. (You have a right to say no and not feel guilty. Just saying you don't like horror movies is enough.)
   - Your teacher assigns a project you don't understand and don't know whether you will be able to do. (You have a right to ask for information. In this case, you could ask for clarification and help so you can do your best work.)
   - Your friends all think it is cool to drive down by the river and drink beer. You've said you'll join them, and now they start to bug you to go along. (You have a right to change your mind. You can tell them you don't think it is cool for you.)
   - A friend borrows your video and returns it broken. You are hurt and angry. (You have a right to experience and express your feelings. You can tell your friend how upset you are and that you would like the video replaced.)
   - Your parent tells you that you can't have an allowance this summer, but you disagree. (You have the right to ask for what you want.)

5. Consider additional examples from the list, encouraging students to generate situations in which their rights might be involved and to figure out what to do in these situations. (Suggest negotiating reasonable alternatives or deciding to insist on your rights.)
6. Discuss the meaning of the phrase "standing up for your rights." What consequences are there for standing up for your rights? What would happen if you insisted on your rights in all situations? Point out that there are some situations in which insisting on your rights wouldn't be a good idea—for example, if you are dealing with a person in authority who is known to be unreasonable and you know asserting yourself would only result in your being hurt in some way.

Closing Time

1. Ask students whether they would be willing to continue to keep track of situations in which they are nonassertive, aggressive, or assertive. Let students know that you will ask for volunteers during the next session to talk about what they noticed about their own behavior.
2. Ask whether there is anything anyone would like to say before the group ends and mention the topic of the next two sessions (choosing a communication style). Remind students of the confidentiality rule and the time for the next meeting.

Personal Rights Handout

You have—

1. The right to act in ways that promote your dignity and self-respect as long as others' rights are not violated in the process
2. The right to be treated with respect
3. The right to say no and not feel guilty
4. The right to experience and express your feelings
5. The right to take time to slow down and think
6. The right to change your mind
7. The right to ask for what you want
8. The right to do less than you are humanly capable of doing
9. The right to ask for information
10. The right to make mistakes
11. The right to feel good about yourself

Note. From *The Assertive Option: Your Rights and Responsibilities* (pp. 80–81), by P. Jakubowski and A. J. Lange, 1978, Champaign, IL: Research Press. Reprinted by permission.

I Have a Choice (Part I)

Goals

1. To continue to reinforce the differences between nonassertive, aggressive, and assertive styles of communication
2. To encourage students to integrate these concepts through active role play so they can exercise more choice in how they behave

Materials

Personal Rights Handout (from Session 2)

Response Discrimination Test

Process

Review

1. Invite students to discuss their experiences in noticing their nonassertive, aggressive, and assertive behaviors. How did they feel in these situations? If they behaved nonassertively or aggressively, what would they have liked to do or say instead?
2. Ask whether group members feel they are presently being denied any of their rights. Allow them to share their ideas, focusing discussion on how it feels when you have rights but don't know how to claim them.

Working Time

1. Briefly describe the goals of the session.
2. Present the idea that we have a *choice* about whether we communicate nonassertively, aggressively, or assertively. Point out that sometimes people act nonassertively or aggressively because they haven't learned the skills to be appropriately assertive. When this is the case, it is difficult for people to get their needs met or their ideas expressed. Ask students whether they have ever felt taken advantage of or misunderstood. Do they think this might have happened because they weren't assertive?
3. Introduce the idea of *role play,* in which people take different parts to illustrate a situation or idea. Explain that you will be using this technique to demonstrate how the three different styles of communication might sound in the following situation. (If you have a co-leader, you can do this role play together. If not, play both parts, switching chairs as you switch roles.)

   Situation: You are asking your friend, Pat, to take your books over to another friend's house so your other friend (Shawn) can use them.

   You: "Pat, would you take these books over to Shawn's house so he can get the homework questions?"

   Pat *(nonassertive):* "Well, oh, all right. I have to be at band practice, but I guess if he has to have them, I might as well go ahead and take them."

   Pat *(aggressive):* "Who do you think I am, your slave?"

   Pat *(assertive):* "Sorry, I can't take the books over to Shawn's house. I have band practice this afternoon."

4. Distribute copies of the Response Discrimination Test, explaining that it is designed to help people *discriminate* (tell the difference between) the three types of communication. Ask students to pair up and take a few minutes to answer the questions on the test. Encourage them to consult the Personal Rights Handout as needed.

5. Go over the answers in the larger group, then invite each of the pairs to choose one of the situations to role play. Their specific assignment is first to role play the response listed on the test, then illustrate the two responses not provided. For example, if the response provided is aggressive, they are to role play it along with nonassertive and assertive responses to the same situation.
6. Give students a few minutes to devise the two new responses, then have them take turns presenting their role plays to the group. Encourage discussion and feedback from group members. Be sure to praise all the players generously.

Closing Time

1. Collect the completed Response Discrimination Tests (these will be used again in Session 4).
2. Ask students whether they can think of a time between now and the next session when they might need to be assertive and whether they would be willing to notice how they respond in this situation. Discuss what group members might hope to achieve by speaking up for themselves and allow group members to share any anxieties they might have about being assertive.
3. Ask whether there is anything anyone would like to say before the group ends and mention the topic of the next session (continued role plays of the situations on the Response Discrimination Test as well as real-life situations). Remind students of the confidentiality rule and the time for the next meeting.

Answer Key

Response Discrimination Test

1. AGG

   Response denies the boy's right to be treated with respect.

   Nonassertive: "Sure. Anything you want."

   Assertive: "I like to choose my hairstyle myself."

2. NON

   Response denies the student's own right to dignity and self-respect.

   Aggressive: "No way! All teachers are unfair."

   Assertive: "OK, Ms. Louis. I'll do the homework over."

3. AST

   Friend appropriately states her right to say no and not feel guilty.

   Nonassertive: "I'm afraid I'll be late for English, but if you want me to, OK."

   Aggressive: "What's the matter with you? Are your arms broken?"

4. AGG

   Steven's response is a deliberate threat to Jerry, not to mention a violation of Jerry's right to be treated with respect. It's true Jerry provoked Steven, but that doesn't mean Steven can ignore Jerry's rights.

   Nonassertive: "Sure, Jerry. Gosh, I'm awful sorry, really."

   Assertive: "I think I have the right to see Luanne if I want to."

5. AGG

   Response violates Marti's right to do less than she is humanly capable of doing.

   Nonassertive: "Oh, dear! It must be my fault for being such a terrible teacher."

   Assertive: "Well, that's too bad."

Answer Key (cont'd)

6. AGG

   Brian's response violates the coach's right to be treated with respect.

   Nonassertive: "Well, um, it'll never happen again, Coach, honest. Please, please don't cut me from the team."

   Assertive: "Sorry, Coach. Ms. Sanders kept me after to help clean up the paints from art class."

7. AST

   Clerk's response is straightforward, not aggressive or self-effacing.

   Nonassertive: "It's all my fault. I should never have sold you that purse."

   Aggressive: "You broke this zipper, didn't you? Well, you're not going to cheat us."

8. NON

   Mr. Peters' response denies his own right to dignity and self-respect.

   Aggressive: "What gives you the right to tell me what to do?"

   Assertive: "We'll quiet down soon, sir."

9. AST

   Girl's response expresses her right to feel good about herself.

   Nonassertive: "I guess I'm just a worthless slob."

   Aggressive: (Punches the first girl.)

10. NON

    The friend acts as though he is unworthy of being thanked, thus denying himself dignity and self-respect.

    Aggressive: "If you weren't such a moron, you wouldn't have left them out in the rain in the first place."

    Assertive: "I'm glad I could help you."

Name____ Date____________________

Response Discrimination Test

Instructions: For each of the situations below, decide whether the response is nonassertive (NON), aggressive (AGG), or assertive (AST). Circle the appropriate answer.

Situation 1
Boy to girlfriend: "I wish you would dye your hair blonde."
Response: "Why don't you go jump in the lake?"
NON AGG AST

Situation 2
Teacher to sixth-grade student: "Your homework is a mess. Do it over."
Student: "Uh, OK, Ms. Louis. I really am a slob."
NON AGG AST

Situation 3
Girl to friend: "Would you get my notebook from my locker for me after math?"
Friend: "Sorry. I can't do it today."
NON AGG AST

Situation 4
Jerry to Steven: "Keep away from Luanne, or I'll make sure you don't have a friend in the school."
Steven: "Just try to make me, and I'll show you who can and can't see Luanne!"
NON AGG AST

Situation 5
Marti to eighth-grade teacher: "Mrs. March, I missed eight spelling words on the last test."
Mrs. March: "Well, what a stupid thing for you to do."
NON AGG AST

Situation 6
Coach to Brian: "Why are you late for practice?"
Brian: "It's none of your darn business."
NON AGG AST

Situation 7
Girl to clerk: "I'd like to return this purse. It's broken here at the zipper."
Clerk: "Would you like a refund or another purse?"
NON AGG AST

Situation 8
Principal to teacher: "Mr. Peters, your class is making too much noise."
Teacher: "Sorry, sir. I really am terribly, awfully sorry, sir."
NON AGG AST

Response Discrimination Test (cont'd)

Situation 9

First girl to second girl: "Why do you wear those beat-up clothes?"
Second girl: "My clothes are my own business."
NON   AGG   AST

Situation 10

Boy to friend: "I'd like to thank you for saving my books from the rain."
Friend: "Gee, gosh, oh, it wasn't anything, really, it was nothing."
NON   AGG   AST

I Have a Choice (Part II)

Goals

1. To continue to reinforce the differences between nonassertive, aggressive, and assertive styles of communication
2. To encourage students to integrate these concepts through active role play
3. To help students apply their understanding of communication style to real-life situations

Materials

Personal Rights Handout (from Session 2)
Response Discrimination Test (from Session 3)

Process

Review

1. Discuss any experiences since the last session in which students assertively expressed their feelings. Were they successful in using appropriate assertion? Did they notice others being assertive? What was the outcome of these situations?

Working Time

1. Briefly describe the goals of the session.
2. Return students' completed Response Discrimination Tests and have them pair up with a different partner from the one they had in Session 3. Instruct each pair to choose another situation to role play. Once again, their task is to illustrate the response given on the test as well as the two alternative responses.
3. After a few minutes, have the pairs present their role plays. Invite discussion, feedback, and positive comments. Encourage students to consult the Personal Rights Handout as needed.
4. When the group has role played the situations on the test, elicit real-life situations in which students either themselves behaved nonassertively, aggressively, or assertively, or observed others doing so. Ask for volunteers to role play these situations, each time illustrating the three styles of communication. Be especially supportive of those students who share personal examples.

Closing Time

1. As a large group, review the pros and cons of each communication style, relating students' personal experiences to the feelings and outcomes associated with these situations. (Refer to the Communicate Straight Chart as needed.)
2. Invite students to continue to observe their own and others' behavior as regards nonassertion, aggression, and assertion.
3. Ask whether there is anything anyone would like to say before the group ends and mention the topic of the next session (expressing positive assertions). Remind students of the confidentiality rule and the time for the next meeting.

Positive Assertions

Goals

1. To introduce the idea that there are three types of assertions: positive, personal rights, and negative
2. To provide practice in giving and receiving positive assertions within the group
3. To encourage students to make positive assertions to people outside the group

Materials

A bag of small pom-pons (can be purchased at most craft shops)
Positive Assertions Record

Process

Review

1. Discuss students' continuing observations of their own and others' use of nonassertive, aggressive, and assertive communication styles.

Working Time

1. Briefly describe the goals of the session.
2. Explain that assertions come in three varieties: positive assertions, personal rights assertions, and negative assertions. Some examples of positive assertions are as follows.
   - I like having you for a friend.
   - You're important to me.
   - Your purple shirt is neat.
   - You were terrific on the team today!
   - We sure are lucky to have you on our squad.
   - I appreciate your help on this paper, Mom.
   - Thanks for the ride, Shawn.
   - I love you!
   - You mean so much to me.
   - You did a great job on your test. Congratulations!
3. Give students a chance to share some examples of positive assertions they've made or heard lately.
4. Discuss how receiving a positive assertion makes a person feel (great, better, needed, like someone cares, etc.). Explain that sometimes positive assertions are called *warm fuzzies* because that's how they make us feel inside. Pass out three pom-pons to each group member, explaining that they are soft and comforting, just like positive assertions.
5. Have group members pair up and instruct them to share three positive assertions with their partners. Encourage them to look beyond physical appearance (e.g., "Your hair is pretty") and try to make comments about other characteristics (e.g., "You have a great sense of humor").
6. After a few minutes, reassemble in the larger group and discuss the following questions.
   - What was it like for you to receive positive assertions from your partner?
   - What was it like to give your partner positive assertions?
   - How do you think your friends, family, or teachers feel when they receive positive assertions?

7. Give each group member a positive assertion yourself. For example: "Sharin, I like how you participated in group today. You're really making excellent progress"; "Amanda, I think you look so attractive in your red sweater"; or "Tyler, your efforts are really paying off."
8. Invite students to share more positive assertions within the group. Each time they give a positive assertion, they are also to give the person a pom-pon, until the three pom-pons they started with are gone. Continue until everyone has had a chance to participate.

Closing Time

1. Distribute the Positive Assertions Record and ask whether students would be willing to make positive assertions to people outside the group and write down their experiences in doing so. Go over the instructions on the form and answer any questions. If students have any pom-pons they received from other group members, invite them to pass these along with their positive assertions.
2. Ask whether there is anything anyone would like to say before the group ends and mention the topic of the next session (standing up for your rights). Remind students of the confidentiality rule and the time for the next meeting.

Name____ Date______________

Positive Assertions Record

Instructions: Fill in the boxes below for each positive assertion you make.

Day	**Person/Rights Involved**	**Person's Response** **Your Thoughts/Feelings**

Stand Up for Your Rights

Goals

1. To reinforce the concept that everyone has basic personal rights and to help students see how these rights work in their own lives
2. To provide an opportunity to discuss situations in which students wish to assert their personal rights
3. To encourage students to make personal rights assertions in appropriate situations outside the group

Materials

Positive Assertions Record (self-improvement exercise from Session 5)

Personal Rights Handout (from Session 2)

Personal Rights Assertions Record

Process

Review

1. Allow members to share information from their completed Positive Assertions Records.

Working Time

1. Briefly describe the goals of the session.
2. Ask students to refer to the Personal Rights Handout. Remind students that assertions come in three varieties: positive assertions, personal rights assertions, and negative assertions. Present the following situations and ask students to say what personal right they think would be involved.
    - Telling your teacher you need help with your homework (right to ask for what you want)
    - Telling your boyfriend to stop tagging along with you between classes and everywhere (right to experience and express your feelings)
    - Asking your dad for more allowance (right to ask for what you want)
    - Asking someone to go out with you (right to ask for what you want)
    - Saying you'd rather not go to a certain party with someone (right to say no and not feel guilty)
3. Encourage students to generate additional examples of situations in which they would like to assert their personal rights but find it difficult to do so. Ask them why they think it is hard to stand up for their rights. Reasons might include the following.
    - Your friends might not like you if you tell them things they don't want to hear.
    - If you make a request, the person might say no.
    - If you've never done it before, standing up for your rights is scary.
    - There aren't any guarantees you'll get what you want just by speaking up.
4. Point out that asserting your personal rights also has some benefits. Elicit the following ideas and encourage students to generate additional ones.
    - If you speak up, at least you have a chance of having your needs met.
    - Other people will respect you more if you don't let them walk all over you.
    - You don't have to keep your feelings inside until you get really angry and blow up.

5. Give a personal example of a time you had to choose whether or not to assert your rights. For example: "I bought some meat from the store, and when I took it home, I discovered it was spoiled. I said to myself, 'Oh, I hate to go back and complain about that meat. They'll probably think I'm a pain in the neck. I'll just throw the meat away. Doggone it!' "
6. Ask students how they think you might feel about throwing the meat away (angry, irritated with yourself). Ask students what personal right(s) you have in the situation. Answers might include the right to experience and express your feelings, the right to ask for what you want, the right to feel good about yourself, and so forth. Elicit that asserting your rights in the situation would involve taking the meat back and asking for a refund. Ask students to help you brainstorm what you might say to the store manager. For example: "This meat is spoiled. I want my money back" or "I'm unhappy with this spoiled meat. I'd like you to exchange it for fresh meat."
7. Invite students to share situations they have faced or will face soon in which they would like to assert their rights. Have the group identify the personal rights involved and brainstorm possible solutions.

Closing Time

1. Distribute the Personal Rights Assertions Record and ask whether students would be willing to practice and record their experiences in asserting their rights with people outside the group. Go over the instructions on the form and answer any questions.
2. Ask whether there is anything anyone would like to say before the group ends and mention the topic of the next session (handling negative assertions). Remind students of the confidentiality rule and the time for the next meeting.

Name______________________________ Date______________

Personal Rights Assertions Record

Instructions: Fill in the boxes below each time you assert your personal rights.

Day	**Person/Rights Involved**	**Person's Response** **Your Thoughts/Feelings**

Negative Assertions

Goals

1. To provide an opportunity to discuss situations in which students wish to make negative assertions
2. To encourage students to make negative assertions in appropriate situations outside the group

Materials

Personal Rights Assertions Record (self-improvement exercise from Session 6)

Negative Assertions Record

Drawing paper

Marking pens in assorted colors

Process

Review

1. Allow members to share information from their completed Personal Rights Assertions Records. Help them determine whether they were appropriately assertive and encourage them to talk about any painful feelings that might have been associated with the experience. (Sometimes group members have been aggressive instead of appropriately assertive. You can also expect to spend some time clarifying the fact that, when you choose to say no, other people may not be used to your asserting yourself and may become angry or confused.)

Working Time

1. Briefly describe the goals of the session.
2. Once again, remind students that assertions come in three varieties: positive assertions, personal rights assertions, and negative assertions. Review the concept that being assertive means expressing your negative feelings, ideas, and beliefs without deliberately hurting other people.
3. Provide the following examples of appropriate negative assertions.
   - Jane borrows Nancy's records and leaves them in the sun on the kitchen table. The records get warped. Jane returns them to Nancy but never bothers to tell her about the warping. Nancy tries to use the records, finds them warped, and is very angry. Nancy says, "Jane, I don't appreciate your borrowing my records and returning them warped. I felt very angry, and I don't want to lend you anything anymore." (Nancy is expressing her justified anger at Jane. Nancy has a right to tell Jane how she feels, and she does so without name-calling or put-downs.)
   - Terry agrees to meet Paul after school at Paul's locker. Paul waits for half an hour, getting more frustrated all the time. Finally, he goes home. He calls Terry and says, "I waited for you for half an hour, missed my bus, and had to walk home. I felt that you weren't respecting my time, and I didn't like that." (Paul is aggravated that Terry inconvenienced him and is letting Terry know of his displeasure in a straightforward, but not hurtful, way.)
   - You have practiced after school for weeks, and now the tryouts for the team are here. You do your best, but you aren't chosen. You go home and tell your parents, "I worked really hard and did the best I could. I feel so disappointed and angry at not being chosen I just don't know what to do." (You're angry and disappointed with yourself for not being chosen, but you express your feelings about the situation openly and honestly.)
4. Ask for volunteers to tell about times they have been angry, irritated, or aggravated by another person or situation. What did they do? Did they feel justified in saying they were upset? How did they feel if they kept their feelings to themselves?

5. Discuss the positive and negative consequences of sharing justified anger.

   Positive consequences

   - The other person involved will know how you honestly feel.
   - You will "clear the air" and not be left feeling resentful.
   - You will gain the respect of the other person because you respected yourself.
   - You will increase your own self-confidence.

   Negative consequences

   - The other person might feel hurt, even though your intention was not to be hurtful.
   - The other person might not like the fact that you are being assertive.
   - If your friendship is not strong, you might lose the friend.

6. Pass out the art materials and ask students whether they would be willing to draw a situation in which they think they could be successful sharing a negative feeling.
7. After giving students a few minutes to finish their drawings, invite them to share their work with the group and explain how they think they might express their negative feeling in an appropriately assertive way. Encourage analysis, feedback, and role playing by group members.

Closing Time

1. Distribute copies of the Negative Assertions Record and ask whether students would be willing to practice and record their experiences in asserting negative feelings with people outside the group. Go over the instructions on the form and answer any questions.
2. Ask whether there is anything anyone would like to say before the group ends and mention the topic of the final session (reviewing what has been learned in the group and saying goodbye). Remind students of the confidentiality rule and the time for the next meeting.

Name________________________________ Date______________

Negative Assertions Record

Instructions: Fill in the boxes below each time you make a negative assertion.

Day	Person/Rights Involved	Person's Response Your Thoughts/Feelings

Saying Goodbye

Goals

1. To provide a review of what has happened in the past seven sessions
2. To help students understand and cope with the fact that the group is ending
3. To illustrate the importance of saying goodbye and give students a chance to achieve closure on the group and their relationships in it

Materials

Negative Assertions Record (self-improvement exercise from Session 7)
Graduation Certificates

Process

Review

1. Invite students to share their experiences in communicating negative assertions, as noted on their completed Negative Assertions Records. Discuss, pointing out that students have spent several years learning to be nonassertive or aggressive and that new behaviors will take a while to learn. Group members will no doubt run into situations in which they will want to be assertive but will not have had enough practice to be comfortable doing so. Praise them for their attempts thus far and encourage them to keep trying.
2. Next, go through the session topics and discuss what students feel are the most important lessons they learned in the group. The following questions may be helpful.
   - What is the difference between nonassertive, aggressive, and assertive styles of communication? (Sessions 1, 3, and 4)
   - What are some of the basic personal rights everyone has? (Session 2)
   - Do you think people have a choice about how they communicate? Which way do you think is best? Why? (Sessions 3 and 4)
   - What are positive assertions? Personal rights assertions? Negative assertions? Why is it important to know how to make these different kinds of assertions? (Sessions 5, 6, and 7)

Working Time

1. Point out that all relationships come to an end, whether by moving away or mutual decision, or for other reasons. Encourage students to talk about their own experiences with having relationships end.
2. Discuss the importance of goodbyes, stressing that saying goodbye can help people deal with sadness when a relationship ends and go on to new relationships.
3. Tell students you are going to model a way of saying goodbye because the group will not be meeting together again and it is the end of a very special relationship. Go around to each student, saying goodbye and remarking on something you learned from him or her. For example:
   - "Maria, I learned that you are a very quiet person but that when you do talk, you have something important to say. I'm going to miss you!"
   - "Saleem, I learned that you really can express yourself assertively and not aggressively. I hope you will come to see me and be my friend in the future."
   - "Kristen, I learned that you can work hard on making changes if you want to. I can see many changes for the better, and I think others appreciate you more now that you are standing up for your rights."

4. Ask students to say goodbye by also saying something positive or encouraging to each individual in the group.

Closing Time

1. Thank students for participating and remind them of the confidentiality rule. Give out the Graduation Certificates and tell students that, even though the group is ending, you will continue to be available to them (if indeed this is the case) and that you hope the friendships made in the group will continue.
2. Encourage students to have a "group hug" if the atmosphere seems right.

Graduate
of Appropriate
Assertions University
I Believe In Me!

Congratulations
to

____

____
Date

Feeling Good about Me: Developing Self-esteem

During the early adolescent years, young people are engaged in a quest to discover their identity. Their world is changing rapidly as they develop biologically, intellectually, and emotionally. These changes in cognitive development allow the young person to deal with abstract ideas such as values, to experience a wider range of emotions, and to explore such psychological aspects of self as personal strengths and weaknesses (Adams & Gullotta, 1989; Harris, 1986). From their interactions with adults and peers, as well as from increased self-insight, youngsters begin to develop a more definite self-concept and to become aware that who they are is strongly related to their sense of self-esteem.

Many influences on self-esteem have been researched. For example, Rosenberg (1965) found higher levels of self-esteem in "crowd members," with the greatest self-esteem being reported among higher status crowds ("jocks" and "populars"). High levels of self-esteem have also been correlated with such factors as positive communication with parents (Walker & Green, 1986) and a sense of having control over one's life, willingness to take moderate risk, and feelings of being an effective person (Gecas, 1982; Rosenberg, 1965). Lower levels of self-esteem have been linked to such factors as excessive parental pressure to succeed in school (Eskilson, Wiley, Muehlbauer, & Doder, 1986); family conflict (Cheung & Lau, 1985); and changing schools (Blyth, Simmons, & Carlton-Ford, 1983). As shown by much of the research in this area, low self-esteem is associated with feelings of anxiety, irritability, depression, alienation, and unhappiness.

The concept of self-esteem is defined by Adams and Gullotta as being "a sense of self-acceptance, a personal liking for one's self and a form of proper respect for oneself" (1989, p. 224). As noted by such authors as Glasser (1969), Dreikurs (1968), and Canfield (1986), the most important aspects of self-esteem are a feeling of belonging or of being needed, a sense of being accepted, and a feeling of being a competent person. Unfortunately, many youths reach early adolescence with a negative self-image and the feeling of "being stuck." Because self-esteem seems to be especially vulnerable during the period from 12 to 14 years, early adolescence is the ideal time for intervention (Simmons, Rosenberg, & Rosenberg, 1973).

Group Objectives

1. To help students discover how they feel about themselves and understand where these perceptions come from
2. To define some of the roles students have in life and to help them see that they perform differently in these various roles
3. To help students become aware of their perceptions of themselves as learners, friends, and persons
4. To help students let go of unrealistic or perfectionistic demands on themselves
5. To encourage students to reinforce other group members for their work on themselves during the group and to learn to receive the same kind of reinforcement

Selection and Other Guidelines

The following target signs may indicate that a student is a candidate for this particular group experience.

1. Hostility, depression, anxiety, irritability, insecurity, or inability to take risks
2. Poor academic performance
3. Poor social and/or personal adjustment
4. Lack of motivation or self-confidence

In addition to following the general selection criteria outlined in the Introduction, choose students with a range of feelings and behaviors with regard to self-esteem. A good mix would be two or three members who are very withdrawn as a result of poor self-image, two or three who express the problem by acting out, and two or three who have fairly good self-esteem but who have other issues or problems relating to self-concept. Even though you might have many candidates for this group, do not select a group of youngsters who are all very low in self-esteem. If all members are lacking in self-esteem, there will be little energy in the group and no positive role models available for the others.

References and Recommended Reading

Adams, G. R., & Gullotta, T. (1989). *Adolescent life experiences.* Belmont, CA: Brooks/Cole.

Blyth, D., Simmons, R., & Carlton-Ford, S. (1983). The adjustment of early adolescents to school transitions. *Journal of Early Adolescence, 3,* 105–120.

Canfield, J. (1986). *Self-esteem in the classroom: A curriculum guide.* Pacific Palisades, CA: Self-Esteem Seminars.

Canfield, J., & Wells, H. (1976). *100 ways to enhance self-concept in the classroom.* Englewood Cliffs, NJ: Erlbaum.

Cheung, P. C., & Lau, S. (1985). Self-esteem: Its relationship to the family and school social environment among Chinese adolescents. *Youth and Society, 14,* 373–387.

Dinkmeyer, D. (1972). *Developing understanding of self and others.* Circle Pines, MN: American Guidance Service.

Dreikurs, R. (1968). *Psychology in the classroom: A manual for teachers* (2nd ed.). New York: Harper and Row.

Eskilson, A., Wiley, G., Muehlbauer, G., & Doder, L. (1986). Parental pressure, self-esteem, and adolescent reported deviance: Bending the twig too far. *Adolescence, 21,* 501–514.

Gecas, V. (1982). The self-concept. *Annual Review of Sociology, 8,* 1–33.

Glasser, W. (1969). *Schools without failure.* New York: Harper and Row.

Harris, L. (1986). *American teens speak: Sex, myths, TV and birth control.* New York: Planned Parenthood.

Jackson, N. F., Jackson, D. A., & Monroe, C. (1983). *Getting along with others.* Champaign, IL: Research Press.

Rosenberg, M. (1965). *Society and the adolescent self-image.* Princeton, NJ: Princeton University Press.

Rosenberg, M. (1985). Self-concept and psychological well-being in adolescence. In R. L. Leaky (Ed.), *The development of the self.* New York: Academic.

Simmons, G. R., Rosenberg, F., & Rosenberg, M. (1973). Disturbances in the self-image at adolescence. *American Sociological Review, 38,* 553–568.

Walker, L. S., & Green, J. W. (1986). The social context of adolescent self-esteem. *Journal of Youth and Adolescence, 15,* 315–322.

Getting Started

Goals

1. To help students become acquainted and feel comfortable in the group setting
2. To choose appropriate ground rules for the group sessions
3. To identify why students want to be a part of the group and what they hope to learn
4. To explore the concept of feelings and to encourage students to begin to express feelings about themselves

Materials

Construction paper name tags, marking pens in assorted colors, straight pins

Paper bag containing several objects having different textures (e.g., eraser, cardboard, magnet, leaf, feather)

Chalkboard or chart paper

Feelings Chart (from the group *Dealing with a Divorce in the Family,* p. 24)

Process

Ice Breaker

1. Welcome students and briefly describe the goals of the group in general as well as this session in particular.
2. Pass out the construction paper name tags and marking pens and ask group members to write down their names, then pin the tags on. Ask them to identify themselves each time they speak during the session so others will learn their names quickly.
3. Tell students you are going to pass around a paper bag with some things in it and that, without looking, they are to feel one item inside the bag and describe it. For example: "I feel something hard, heavy, and cold" or "I feel something light and soft." Let each group member take a turn.
4. Ask students to tell what it was like to feel and describe the different objects. Allow them to share their responses—that they felt strange, funny, amused, and so forth. Inform them that during the next several group sessions they will be working on identifying how they feel about different aspects of themselves, just as they identified the different objects in the bag. Point out that when you know how you feel about something it is easier to make changes to improve yourself.

Working Time

1. Introduce the idea of ground rules, pointing out that rules help everyone be respected and have time to talk. Suggest a few basic ground rules, such as the following.
   - What we say and do here is private and stays in the group (confidentiality rule).
   - Everyone has the right to "pass"—that is, not to participate in an activity or part of an activity.
   - No fighting or arguing.
   - Each person gets time to talk.
   - When someone is talking, everyone else will listen.
2. Ask students to think of other ground rules for the group. List all rules on the chalkboard or on chart paper.
3. Distribute a copy of the Feelings Chart to each student. Explain that feelings are a very special part of us and that they come in varying intensities, as shown on the chart. They could be called the "spice of life" because they are what keep us interested and in touch with what is going on in our world. Point out that feelings are neither good nor bad and that it is important to share feelings in an appropriate way. Feelings don't go away when you keep them inside—in fact, they sometimes get worse.

4. Encourage students to discuss the following questions.
   - Could you talk about some of your feelings about being here in this group? What do you hope to learn?
   - How scary do you think it is to trust other group members with your feelings? What would make doing this less scary?
   - Would it be OK to talk about some feelings and keep some feelings to yourself? What feelings would be OK to talk about?
   - Which of these feelings do you have frequently? Which do you want to have more often?

Closing Time

1. Invite students to discuss what they found out about themselves today and what it was like to hear about how others felt. Share some positive observations about each group member. For example: "Russell, you really seem ready to talk about how you feel about yourself" or "That was a good idea you had for a ground rule, Jeanne."
2. Ask whether there is anything anyone would like to say before the group ends and mention the topic of the next session (what we like and dislike about ourselves). Remind students of the confidentiality rule and the time for the next meeting.

What I Like and Dislike about Me

Goals

1. To help students identify what they like and dislike about themselves
2. To encourage students to feel comfortable expressing their feelings with a partner
3. To illustrate that how students see themselves may not necessarily be how others see them

Materials

Likes and Dislikes Worksheet

Process

Review

1. Invite students to bring up any questions or comments from the last session and ask them to discuss what they think so far about sharing information concerning their feelings. Are they comfortable doing so? What do they think might make them more at ease?

Working Time

1. Briefly describe the goals of the session.
2. Distribute copies of the Likes and Dislikes Worksheet and ask students to spend a few minutes filling it out.
3. When students have finished, have them pair up. Each member of the pair takes a turn introducing items from the worksheet with the phrase "I am a person who . . . " For example: "I am a person who likes the way I can cook lasagna." Encourage students to make additional statements about things they have not written on their worksheets.
4. Reassemble in the larger group to discuss the following questions.
   - Do you have more things written down in the likes or dislikes column?
   - What do you like about yourself? Does anyone else in the group like the same thing?
   - What do you do well by yourself? With friends?
   - What is one of your successes? When are you at your best?
   - Whom do you pretend to be? Wish you were? Hope you can become?
   - What do you dislike about yourself? Is that something you would like to change? Why?
5. During this discussion, encourage students to challenge the negative statements they hear group members making about themselves and to suggest ways the "dislike" could be changed into a "like." For example: "Sara, you could get a permanent if you dislike your straight hair" or "Logan, you said you think you will never make it to college because you don't like school. How do you know if you've never given it a try?"
6. Allow group members to process this information for as long as they need. It is very important for students to hear themselves described and affirmed by the leader and others.

Closing Time

1. Invite students to explain what they learned about themselves from this session and to give a positive description of themselves in three words. For example: "I am capable, a good worker, and treat people kindly" or "I am a good sport, dress sharp, and have a great smile."
2. Ask whether students would be willing to take their Likes and Dislikes Worksheet home and think of more things they like about themselves. They can also write down the group's suggestions and any other ideas they might have for changing their dislikes into likes.
3. Ask whether there is anything anyone would like to say before the group ends and mention the topic of the next session (different roles people have). Remind students of the confidentiality rule and the time for the next meeting.

Name____ Date____________________

Likes and Dislikes Worksheet

Instructions: Write down some of the things you like and dislike about yourself in the columns below. Then write down some ways you could change your "dislikes" into "likes."

Likes	***Dislikes***
1. ______________________	1. ______________________
______________________	______________________
2. ______________________	2. ______________________
______________________	______________________
3. ______________________	3. ______________________
______________________	______________________
4. ______________________	4. ______________________
______________________	______________________
5. ______________________	5. ______________________
______________________	______________________

What are some ways I can change my "dislikes" into "likes?"

1. ____
2. ____
3. ____
4. ____
5. ____

Everyone Has Roles

Goals

1. To help students understand that they have many different roles in life
2. To encourage students to explore how they feel about themselves in three of these roles: as learners, friends, and persons (both emotional and physical aspects)
3. To illustrate that people may feel differently about their performance in these various roles

Materials

Roles Questionnaire

Process

Review

1. Ask students whether they added anything new that they liked about themselves to their Likes and Dislikes Worksheet and whether they were able to think of any new ways to change their dislikes about themselves into likes. Use open-ended questions to discuss.

Working Time

1. Briefly describe the goals of the session.
2. Ask students to define the term *role* (a part or function assumed by someone, like a part in a play). Explain that each of us has a number of different roles as a result of our age, occupation, gender, or other aspects of self. For example, Ms. Schultz is in the role of principal at school, but when she goes home she is in the role of wife and mother. When she goes to visit her parents, she is in the role of daughter. (One way to explain this concept is to ask students to imagine what different hats a person might wear.)
3. Encourage students to identify the various roles they assume: student, son or daughter, friend, team member, grandchild, club member, scout, choir member, 4-H member, and so forth. Point out that we probably think we do well in some roles and not so well in others.
4. Distribute copies of the Roles Questionnaire and explain that this form is designed to help people understand how they feel about themselves in three different roles: learner, friend, and person. Allow students a few minutes to complete the questionnaire.
5. Have students pair up and invite them to share some of their feelings about themselves in the three roles.
6. Reassemble in the larger group and discuss the following questions.

   Learner

   - What are some of the ways you see yourself as a learner or student?
   - How do you think you got this picture of yourself?
   - How much does your behavior (what you do or don't do) have to do with your picture of yourself as a student?
   - How much do the opinions of other people (parents, friends, or teachers) affect you?

   Friend

   - Overall, what do you think of yourself as a friend?
   - If you were someone else, would you like to have yourself as a friend?
   - What kind of a friend would you like to be?

Person

- What do you like about yourself as a person?
- What areas would you like to change?
- What kind of person would you like others to say you are?

7. The following general questions may also be helpful.
   - Was filling out the questionnaire easy? Difficult?
   - Did you feel better about yourself in some roles and worse in others? If so, why do you think this is?
   - Did your partner feel the same way you did about these roles? What differences did you discover? Why do you think these differences exist?
   - What was it like to talk about your feelings to your partner?
   - Were you surprised about anything that happened in the group today?

Closing Time

1. Collect the questionnaires from students (these will be used again in Session 4). Invite students to continue to think about what roles they play and how they feel about themselves in each of them.
2. Ask whether there is anything anyone would like to say before the group ends and mention the topic of the next session (setting goals as a learner). Remind students of the confidentiality rule and the time for the next meeting.

Name____ Date____________________

Roles Questionnaire

Instructions: Circle the number that best represents how you see yourself in the following roles. Numbers 1 and 2 mean you see yourself as being more like the word on the left. Numbers 4 and 5 mean you see yourself as being more like the word on the right. Number 3 means you see yourself as being in the middle.

How I Feel about Myself as a Learner

1. unsuccessful	1	2	3	4	5	successful
2. unsatisfied	1	2	3	4	5	satisfied
3. shaky	1	2	3	4	5	sure
4. worse than others	1	2	3	4	5	better than others
5. bored	1	2	3	4	5	stimulated
6. aggravated with school	1	2	3	4	5	satisfied with school
7. poor study skills	1	2	3	4	5	good study skills
8. weak test taker	1	2	3	4	5	strong test taker
9. disliked by teachers	1	2	3	4	5	liked by teachers
10. angry with school	1	2	3	4	5	happy with school

How I Feel about Myself as a Friend

1. insecure	1	2	3	4	5	secure
2. criticized	1	2	3	4	5	accepted
3. ignored	1	2	3	4	5	wanted
4. powerless	1	2	3	4	5	strong
5. friendless	1	2	3	4	5	many friends
6. inferior	1	2	3	4	5	superior
7. poor friendship skills	1	2	3	4	5	good friendship skills
8. despised	1	2	3	4	5	loved
9. unpopular	1	2	3	4	5	popular
10. ashamed	1	2	3	4	5	proud

Roles Questionnaire (cont'd)

How I Feel about Myself as a Person

My Emotions

1. uncaring	1	2	3	4	5	caring
2. dishonest	1	2	3	4	5	honest
3. insensitive	1	2	3	4	5	sensitive
4. impatient	1	2	3	4	5	patient
5. unfriendly	1	2	3	4	5	friendly
6. unhappy	1	2	3	4	5	happy
7. depressed	1	2	3	4	5	joyful
8. rejected	1	2	3	4	5	accepted
9. scared	1	2	3	4	5	confident
10. incompetent	1	2	3	4	5	competent

My Physical Self

1. not good looking	1	2	3	4	5	very good looking
2. too short	1	2	3	4	5	tall enough
3. too thin	1	2	3	4	5	right weight
4. too heavy	1	2	3	4	5	right weight
5. uncoordinated	1	2	3	4	5	good coordination
6. not grown up enough	1	2	3	4	5	grown up enough
7. bad complexion	1	2	3	4	5	nice complexion
8. weak	1	2	3	4	5	strong
9. dislike my nose	1	2	3	4	5	like my nose
10. dislike my hair	1	2	3	4	5	like my hair

My Goals as a Learner

Goals

1. To illustrate that setting learning goals can help students improve their self-image
2. To help students set specific goals for how they would like to be as learners

Materials

Roles Questionnaire (from Session 3)
Red pens or pencils

Process

Review

1. Ask students whether they can remember some of the roles mentioned in Session 3. Were they able to think of any additional roles they play? If so, do they feel they perform each of these roles equally well, or do they play some better than others?

Working Time

1. Briefly describe the goals of the session.
2. Pass back students' completed Roles Questionnaires along with the red pens or pencils. Instruct students to pretend that for a year they can have unlimited access to all of the resources imaginable to improve themselves as learners. Encourage students to go beyond academic learning and think of learning in all facets of life: sports, music, drama, art, and so forth. Then ask them to use their red pens or pencils to rate how they would feel about themselves after that year had passed.
3. After giving students a few minutes to complete this task, explain that these hopes for the future are students' *goals*. Brainstorm some ways to reach these goals. For example:
   - Go to a workshop on test-taking skills.
   - Ask your teacher for extra help.
   - Ask a friend who is a good student to study with you.
   - Ask the coach to give you some pointers.
   - Set aside 20 minutes a day to work on a certain project.
   - Find out how the local library can help you.
   - Take lessons (music, art, dancing, etc.).
   - Learn relaxation techniques to help you calm down during tests.
   - Put projects on a time schedule.
   - Reward yourself for short-term achievements.
4. Ask students to imagine where they would be a year from now if they hadn't set any goals (in about the same place they are now). Then invite them to select from the list (or generate on their own) three ways they think would best help them reach their learning goals. Encourage them to tell which methods they choose and to explain how they think these methods will help.
5. Collect the Roles Questionnaires from students (these will be used again in Session 5).

Closing Time

1. Wrap up the session by discussing the following questions.
   - What are you aware of now that you weren't aware of when you came to group today?
   - How many of you believe you could do better in school if you worked towards your goals?
   - When do you think you will get going to do something about your goals?
2. Ask whether there is anything anyone would like to say before the group ends and mention the topic of the next session (exploring friendship goals). Remind students of the confidentiality rule and the time for the next meeting.

Exploring Friendship Goals

Goals

1. To reinforce the concept that setting goals can help students improve their self-image
2. To help students set specific goals for how they would like to be as friends

Materials

Roles Questionnaire (from Session 3)
Red pens or pencils

Process

Review

1. Remind students that during the last session they identified goals for themselves as learners, whether in school or in sports, music, skills, games, or other activities. They then brainstormed ways to reach those goals. Ask students whether they had a chance to put any of these methods to use and, if so, what the results were. Discuss.

Working Time

1. Pass back students' completed Roles Questionnaires along with the red pens or pencils. Instruct students to pretend once again that they have unlimited access for a year to everything that would help them feel better about themselves as friends. Then ask them to use their red pens or pencils to mark their questionnaires to show how they would like to feel about themselves.
2. Point out that these changes reflect the students' *goals* for the future. Invite students to brainstorm ways they might reach these goals. For example:
   - Learn how to start a conversation with a new person.
   - Practice offering to help someone who might become a friend.
   - Learn how to avoid situations that look like trouble.
   - Volunteer to help someone study for a test.
   - Invite someone to eat lunch with you.
   - Help someone learn a new skill or game.
   - Stick up for your friends (be loyal).
   - Learn how to negotiate differences.
   - Practice giving compliments.
   - Smile and use good eye contact when talking with others.
3. Ask students to select from this list (or generate on their own) five ways they think would best help them feel better about themselves as friends. Invite students to tell which methods they choose and to explain how they think these methods will help them reach their friendship goals. The following discussion questions may be helpful.
   - What do you think others say about you as a friend?
   - Do you think other people's image of you is really the way you are?
   - If you could change people's image of you, what would you most want to change?
   - Are you willing to change your behavior so others will be more receptive to you?

Closing Time

1. Collect the Roles Questionnaires from students (these will be used a final time in Session 6).
2. Ask whether there is anything anyone would like to say before the group ends and mention the topic of the next session (reaching personal goals). Remind students of the confidentiality rule and the time for the next meeting.

Reaching Personal Goals

Goals

1. To help students set specific goals for how they would like to feel about their emotional and physical selves
2. To illustrate the idea that you can change how you feel about yourself as a person by changing what you think
3. To clarify what aspects of one's emotional and physical self can and cannot be changed

Materials

Roles Questionnaire (from Session 3)

Red pens or pencils

Chalkboard or chart paper

Process

Review

1. Remind students that during the last two sessions they identified goals for themselves as learners and as friends. They then brainstormed ways to reach those goals. Ask students to share what experiences they might have had in putting these methods to use.

Working Time

1. Pass back students' completed Roles Questionnaires along with the red pens or pencils. Ask them to use their red pens or pencils to mark their questionnaires to show what goals they might have for themselves in terms of how they feel about themselves as persons (both emotional and physical aspects).
2. On chalkboard or chart paper, make three columns. Over the first column, put an *A* and explain that this column is for situations in which students experience certain feelings about themselves that they would prefer not to have. Ask students to generate a number of these situations. Responses might include the following.
   - I feel really depressed when no one sits next to me at lunch.
   - I feel incompetent when the teacher calls on me and I don't know the answer.
   - I just hate my hair. I look like a dog.
   - I feel really scared when the teacher calls on me in class.
3. Over the second column, put a *B* and explain that this column is for the thoughts you have about the situation. Elicit several thoughts that might pertain to one of the situations described. For example, the student who sits alone at lunch might be thinking the situation is really awful or that being alone at lunch means he or she will never have any friends.
4. Over the third column, put a *C*. Explain that this column is for the feelings associated with the situation. Ask students how they think they would feel if no one sat next to them at lunch and they had the thoughts they described about the situation. Responses might include "really bummed out," "like crying," and so forth.
5. Ask students what they think causes these feelings. Most will respond that having to sit alone at lunch (*A*) causes them to feel depressed (*C*). Challenge this belief by inviting students to change the thoughts in the *B* column to more moderate ones. For example: "So what if I'm sitting alone at lunch—I have a friend in algebra class"; "It's not the end of the world that I don't have as many friends as I'd like"; or "Maybe I could strike up a conversation with that new kid." Ask students whether they would still feel as depressed if they changed their thoughts about the situation in this way.

6. Point out that situations (*A*'s) don't cause feelings (*C*'s) but that thoughts (*B*'s) cause feelings: No one forces us to feel a certain way about ourselves in any particular situation. Suggest the idea that, if you can change what you think about yourself in a situation, you can also change how you feel.
7. Explain that using this technique can be especially helpful in dealing with physical characteristics that are out of your control. For example, if it really bothers you that you are too tall, there's not much you can do to become shorter, but you could stop telling yourself it is terrible to be so tall and try focusing on your positive qualities instead.
8. Guide students in a discussion of what physical aspects they think they can change and what aspects they think they will have to accept. For example:
   - If you dislike your hair, you could get a different style.
   - If you think you are too tall, you will probably have to learn to accept this about yourself.
   - If you think you are too fat or too thin, you could see the school nurse or your family physician for advice on diet.
   - If you think you are uncoordinated, you could take dance or karate lessons.
   - If you hate your nose, you could learn make-up techniques and hairstyles to minimize its size, save up for a nose job, or just learn to like your nose.
   - If you think your feet are too big, you will probably have to learn to live with them the way they are.
   - If you think you have a bad complexion, you could see a dermatologist or just wait until your skin gets better on its own.
   - If you dislike having freckles, you could use make-up or you could learn to like them.

Closing Time

1. Invite students to think seriously about the personal goals they have. How do they plan to reach these goals? Do they think they will try the technique illustrated in this session to help them deal with unpleasant feelings? Which things about themselves do they think they will just have to accept?
2. Ask whether there is anything anyone would like to say before the group ends and mention the topic of the next session (avoiding perfectionistic thinking). Remind students of the confidentiality rule and the time for the next meeting.

Perfect in Every Way

Goals

1. To help students recognize perfectionistic beliefs
2. To illustrate that perfection is impossible and unnecessary
3. To encourage students to challenge perfectionistic thinking in themselves and other group members

Materials

Select 3–4 from the following groups of objects: pictures of Presidents of the United States, movie stars, baseball players, or Nobel prize winners; eggs; marbles; or other slightly different items of the same class or type

Process

Review

1. Invite students to share which aspects of their emotional or physical selves they have decided to work on and to discuss the methods they have chosen for reaching their goals. Have students tried changing their thinking about situations in order to change how they feel about themselves? If so, what was the outcome? What other ideas have they tried?

Working Time

1. Briefly describe the goals of the session.
2. Place the items chosen on a table and instruct the group to come up and examine them very carefully. After the students have had a chance to study the items, ask the following questions (modified to suit the items chosen):
   - Which of the Presidents do you think was the most perfect President?
   - Which one of the eggs is the most perfect egg?
   - Which one of the marbles is the most perfect example of a marble?
   - Which movie star is the greatest, the most perfect of all movie stars?
3. Ask students whether they know why they are attempting to find the best example from the different groups of items. Elicit the fact that there are many "bests" and no one example from these groups is absolutely perfect. The following discussion questions may be helpful.
   - How many perfect people have you met in your lifetime?
   - If you haven't met a perfect person, what do you think your chances are of meeting one in the future?
   - Do you think it is possible to be perfect? What would being perfect be like?
4. Point out that since being perfect is impossible (and even if it were possible, wouldn't be much fun), it doesn't make much sense for us to think we have to be perfect to be liked, wanted, successful, or happy. Ask students to share some perfectionistic ideas that might keep them from feeling good about themselves. For example:
   - If I don't get all *A*'s, I'm no good.
   - If I'm not beautiful/handsome, no one will ever go out with me.
   - If I'm clumsy, everyone will laugh at me.
   - If I don't get on the team, I'll never be able to face my friends.
   - If I'm not smart, I'll never get a good job.

5. Discuss the following questions.
   - Do you think you were born with perfectionistic ideas, or did you learn them?
   - Can you remember a time when you might not have had these perfectionistic ideas? What do you think might have happened to change you?
   - Do you think it is possible for your ideas about yourself to change again in the future?

   Stress that one's self-image is not cast in concrete and that if students' ideas about themselves changed once, they can change again.

6. Bring up the idea that students can help one another develop positive self-esteem by challenging perfectionistic ideas in the group. For example:
   - "Jerry, just because you didn't make the team doesn't mean you're no good at anything. Look how you make us all laugh!"
   - "Pam, you seemed embarrassed after telling us you get *D*'s in science. It's painful to let others know about unpleasant things, but you're doing the best you can."

Closing Time

1. Ask whether students would be willing to challenge perfectionistic thinking in themselves and in other group members when they see it.
2. Ask whether there is anything anyone would like to say before the group ends and mention the topic of the final session (reviewing what has been learned in the group and saying goodbye). Remind students of the confidentiality rule and the time for the next meeting.

Saying Goodbye

Goals

1. To provide a review of what has happened in the past seven sessions
2. To help students understand and cope with the fact that the group is ending
3. To illustrate the importance of saying goodbye and give students a chance to achieve closure on the group and their relationships in it

Materials

Nutritious snack for everyone (raisins, fruit drink, etc.)

Process

Review

1. Ask students whether they were able to recognize perfectionistic thinking in themselves or in other people. How did it feel to observe this kind of thinking? What did students do to try to challenge it?
2. Next, go through the session topics and discuss what students feel are the most important lessons they learned in the group. The following questions may be helpful.
   - What did you learn about your likes and dislikes about yourself? (Session 2)
   - What kinds of roles can a person have? Do you think everyone is equally pleased with all of these possible roles? (Session 3)
   - What goals did you set for yourself as a learner? How do you plan to reach them? (Session 4)
   - What goals did you set for yourself as a friend? How and when do you plan to get started on them? (Session 5)
   - What goals did you set for yourself as a person (both emotional and physical aspects)? How can changing what you think about yourself change how you feel? Is there anything about yourself you can't change? (Session 6)
   - What is perfectionistic thinking? Do you think you have to be perfect in everything to be a good person? (Session 7)

Working Time

1. Point out that all relationships come to an end, whether by moving away or mutual decision, or for other reasons. Discuss the importance of goodbyes, stressing that saying goodbye can help people deal with sadness when a relationship ends and go on to new relationships.
2. Model saying something encouraging about each student as a way of saying goodbye, then encourage other group members to do the same. For example:
   - "Jill, you've really accomplished some of your personal goals. I'm pleased to see you working on yourself."
   - "Diana, even though you had a difficult time getting started, you kept coming to group. I appreciate that very much."
   - "Brian, I know talking about personal things was very hard for you. I hope you feel better now that you've reached some of your goals."

Closing Time

1. Remind students of the confidentiality rule. Thank them for participating and tell them that, even though the group is ending, you will continue to be available to them (if this is indeed the case) and that you wish them success in reaching their goals to improve their self-esteem.
2. Encourage students to have a "group hug" if the atmosphere seems right, then enjoy the snacks.

Keeping Your Cool: Stress Management Skills

Adults in our society are bombarded with information on stress and how to manage it. There are dozens of support groups for the situations that cause stress, numerous stress management seminars and workshops sponsored by local social service agencies and mental health centers, and countless magazine articles giving advice and instruction on how to deal with stress. Children, on the other hand, receive little or no information on what stress is or how to deal with it. Perhaps we believe that young people don't experience stress or that they don't have the worries adults do. Sadly, such perceptions can keep many youths from getting the assistance they need before they wind up on crisis' doorstep.

Significant changes in society have caused increased pressure on the younger part of our population. Some of the most commonly occurring stressful situations for this group are family turmoil and divorce, frequent moves, peer pressure to become involved in illegal activity, adult pressure to succeed academically or athletically, and illness and/or injury (Medeiros, Porter, & Welch, 1983). Without sufficient family support and coping skills, the young person has a heavy burden indeed.

Among the techniques available to help both adults and youngsters cope with stress are progressive muscle relaxation (Benson, 1976; Bernstein & Borkovec, 1973; Cautela & Groden, 1978) and clinically standardized meditation (Carrington, 1978; Throll, 1982). Progressive muscle relaxation has been demonstrated to be effective in helping youths reduce and control nonattending behaviors (Redfering & Bowman, 1981), decreasing test anxiety in test-anxious middle school children (Smead, 1981), and calming anxious mildly mentally handicapped middle school youths (Morganett & Bauer, 1987).

As human beings, we respond to stress according to our own learning experiences, coping skills, and support systems. Youngsters have less of all of the above than adults and are more likely to respond in whatever way is most immediately available. Abuse of drugs and alcohol is one available response, as are depression and self-destructive behavior. Some young adolescents act out their frustrations in socially inappropriate ways, even becoming involved with the juvenile justice system, whereas others internalize the pressures put upon them, becoming more angry, withdrawn, and out of touch with those around them (Elkind, 1982; Hammond, 1979; Kaplan, 1970).

More subtle ways of dealing with stress can be readily observed in any school classroom or hallway: hostility and irritability, low frustration tolerance, bullying, underachievement, and so forth. Although we may not identify stress as the immediate cause of many of these problems, teaching ways to reduce and cope with stress may be a successful way of eliminating these behaviors (Selye, 1977).

Group Objectives

1. To promote understanding of the stress response and individual stressors
2. To encourage awareness of how stressors affect us physically, psychologically, and behaviorally
3. To teach three main techniques for managing stress: progressive muscle relaxation, guided imagery, and positive coping statements
4. To help students see that stress can be reduced and to encourage them to practice stress management techniques both inside and outside of the group setting

Selection and Other Guidelines

The following target signs may indicate that a student is a candidate for this particular group experience.

1. Recent life change, such as moving, family disruption, or loss of friends
2. High pressure to perform academically, athletically, or socially
3. Poor skills for coping with peer pressure
4. Nervousness, anxiousness, or irritability in exam situations or in other circumstances
5. Repetitive behaviors (e.g., foot tapping, finger drumming), stuttering, teeth grinding, or trembling
6. Unusual aggressiveness or laziness
7. Increase in accidents ("accident-proneness")
8. Bed-wetting, nightmares, insomnia, or indigestion

In addition to following the general guidelines outlined in the Introduction and looking for these signs, it is helpful to administer the Children's State-Trait Anxiety Inventory (STAIC). [1] By using this standardized test, you can obtain a measure of anxiety level and thus ensure that the members selected are truly in need of the group experience. This measure can also help you constitute the group so that a range of abilities in handling stress is represented. A good mix would include four or five members who exhibit very high anxiety levels and four or five whose anxiety scores are more moderate. The goal is to include at least a few students who can model some positive skills and attitudes.

You could also select group members based on significant life events that appear to be unresolved sources of stress. Examples might include a family divorce, move, death of a significant person, failure experience, and so forth. If you use life events as criteria, avoid selecting students who are presently in a state of crisis and keep in mind that stress reactions to such events are highly individual. For example, not all children from families experiencing divorce exhibit high levels of stress; the perception of stress may well be the adult's and not the child's. For this reason, use of the STAIC is recommended.

References and Recommended Reading

Benson, H. (1976). *The relaxation response.* New York: Avon.

Bernstein, D. A., & Borkovec, T. D. (1973). *Progressive relaxation training: A manual for the helping professions.* Champaign, IL: Research Press.

Carrington, P. (1978). *Clinically standardized meditation* (Instructor's Manual). Kendall Park, NJ: Pace Educational Systems.

Cautela, J. R., & Groden, J. (1978). *Relaxation: A comprehensive manual for adults, children, and children with special needs.* Champaign, IL: Research Press.

Cormier, W. H., & Cormier, L. S. (1985). *Interviewing strategies for helpers.* Monterey, CA: Brooks/Cole.

Curtis, J. D., & Detert, R. A. (1981). *How to relax: A holistic approach to stress management.* Palo Alto, CA: Mayfield.

Davis, M., McKay, M., & Eshelman, E. R. (1982). *The relaxation and stress reduction workbook* (2nd ed.). Oakland, CA: New Harbinger.

Elkind, D. (1982). *The hurried child.* New York: Addison-Wesley.

Hammond, J. M. (1979). Children of divorce: A study of self-concept, academic achievement, and attitudes. *The Elementary School Journal, 80,* 55–62.

Hosford, R. (1974). *Counseling techniques* (Self-as-Model Film). Washington, DC: Personnel and Guidance Press.

Kaplan, B. L. (1970). Anxiety: A classroom close-up. *The Elementary School Journal, 71,* 70–77.

McKay, M., Davis, M., & Fanning, P. (1981). *Thoughts and feelings: The art of cognitive stress intervention.* Oakland, CA: New Harbinger.

Medeiros, D. C., Porter, B. J., & Welch, I. D. (1983). *Children under stress.* Englewood Cliffs, NJ: Prentice-Hall.

Meichenbaum, D. (1985). *Stress-inoculation training.* Elmsford, NY: Pergamon.

Merzfeld, G., & Powell, R. (1986). *Coping for kids: A complete stress-control program for students ages 8–18.* West Nyack, NY: Center for Applied Research in Education.

Morganett, R. S., & Bauer, A. M. (1987). Coping strategies in mainstreaming educable mentally handicapped children. *Indiana Counsel for Exceptional Children Quarterly, 36,* 20–24.

Redfering, D. L., & Bowman, M. J. (1981). Effects of a meditative relaxation exercise on non-attending behaviors of behaviorally disturbed children. *Journal of Clinical Child Psychology, 10,* 126–127.

Selye, H. (1956). *The stress of life* (rev. ed.). New York: McGraw-Hill.

[1] This measure is available from Consulting Psychologists Press, 577 College Avenue, Palo Alto, CA 94306-1490.

Selye, H. (1977, November). How to master stress. *Parents Magazine,* 25–35.

Smead, R. (1981). *A comparison of counselor administered and tape-recorded relaxation training on decreasing target and non-target anxiety in elementary school children.* Unpublished doctoral dissertation, Auburn University.

Throll, D. A. (1982). Transcendental meditation and progressive relaxation: Their physiological effects. *Journal of Clinical Psychology, 38,* 522–530.

Getting Started

Goals

1. To help students become acquainted, begin to feel comfortable in the group setting, and identify what they hope to learn
2. To choose appropriate ground rules for the group sessions
3. To define stress and to introduce the concept of the stress response

Materials

Chalkboard or chart paper

Process

Ice Breaker

1. Welcome students and briefly describe the goals of the group in general as well as this session in particular.
2. Instruct students to pair up with the person next to them and share the following information: name, something that causes you a lot of stress, something stressful that you handle pretty well, and what you hope to learn from the group. Tell students that they will be introducing their partners and sharing the information they learned when the group reassembles.
3. After a few minutes, regroup and have members introduce their partners by name and share their partners' information about stress and what they hope to learn from the group.
4. Praise students for sharing personal information, explaining that you understand it can be risky to tell something about yourself to others but that expressing your thoughts and feelings to others can help you understand who you are.

Working Time

1. Introduce the idea of ground rules, pointing out that rules help everyone be respected and have time to talk. Suggest a few basic ground rules, such as the following.
   - What we say and do here is private and stays in the group (confidentiality rule).
   - Everyone has the right to "pass"—that is, not to participate in an activity or part of an activity.
   - No fighting or arguing.
   - Each person gets time to talk.
   - When someone is talking, everyone else will listen.
2. Ask students to think of other ground rules for the group. List all rules on the chalkboard or on chart paper.
3. Ask students what they think *stress* is and encourage them to discuss their ideas. Explain that one dictionary definition of stress is "a force exerted on a body that tends to deform its shape." If you take an iron bar and stress it—that is, stretch it or press it too much—it will change its shape.
4. Use some of the examples generated by students in the ice breaker to illustrate the point that, if things happen in our lives that are too much for us to deal with, then we also tend to "get out of shape" or behave differently than we usually do. For example, if someone starts calling you names, you might feel so stressed and angry that you would hit the name-caller or do something else you wouldn't ordinarily do. Invite students to share examples of situations in which they felt so stressed that they did or said something uncharacteristic.

5. Next, explain that you will be conducting a "guided fantasy." Instruct students to close their eyes and picture the following story.

   You are back in prehistoric times. Sabre-toothed tigers and great wooly mammoths are roaming the land. You are standing on top of a cliff, watching a small band of people dressed in skins grouped around a fire. They are warming themselves and eating food that they hunted that day. The women are feeding the young children. Because life is so dangerous, they must be on guard constantly. Their home is the cave at the bottom of the cliff where you are now standing.

   Off in the distance, a huge sabre-toothed tiger, bigger than any tiger alive today, smells the food the people around the fire are eating. He is ravenously hungry and begins running toward the people. A man on guard at the edge of the group sees the tiger as it runs toward them. He shouts and screams to the people around the fire. Terror strikes their hearts! Their lives are in danger. What should they do? What can they do to protect themselves? They have only crude spears that would be no match against the powerful tiger. They have only two choices to save themselves: They can *fight* with the weapons they have, or they can *run* into their cave and hide. They can fight, or they can run. Fight or run. Fight or run.

   On top of the cliff, you can see the prehistoric people running in panic. Their hearts have started pumping faster in order to carry more blood and oxygen to their legs for running, climbing, and fighting. The pupils of their eyes open wider to let in more light for seeing better. The palms of their hands perspire. The hormone adrenaline is pumped into their bloodstreams, giving them enormous energy. These and other changes in the body are called the *stress response.* The body responds to danger and threat by getting ready to fight or run, the only two choices the cave people have to save themselves. The stress response helps them because it makes the body function at its highest potential. When danger occurs, the stress response occurs.

   You watch as the prehistoric people run toward their cave, scrambling up to the highest ledges and grabbing their spears and feeding the fire to keep the tiger out. The tiger retreats, knowing the fire is dangerous. The cave people are safe once again.

6. Tell students the guided fantasy is over and instruct them to open their eyes. Discuss the following questions.

   - What happened when the cave people found out they were in great danger? *(stress response)*
   - What happens to your body when you have the stress response?
   - Do we still have the stress response today, even though we don't have sabre-toothed tigers after us?
   - Do we have a choice between running and fighting? What does that mean today? *(getting away from a stressful situation or staying and getting involved)*
   - Do we have situations that threaten our lives? What might these be?
   - What kinds of situations don't actually threaten our lives but are threatening in other ways, perhaps to our self-confidence or self-esteem?
   - What kinds of reactions do you have when you are stressed? Point out in discussing these questions that stress can be caused by things happening outside ourselves, such as going to the dentist, being threatened by a bully, and so forth. Things that happen inside ourselves can also cause stress—for example, thinking about the possibility of failure or worrying about a future unpleasant situation.

Closing Time

1. Ask students to explain what they learned in the session. Elicit the idea that, even though times have changed, our bodies haven't changed that much and they still respond to danger with the stress response.
2. Encourage students to think about the stressful situations they find themselves in outside of the group and to monitor their own stress response. How do their bodies change when they are under stress? Do they feel like fighting or running?
3. Ask whether there is anything anyone would like to say before the group ends and mention the topic of the next session (understanding what kinds of things cause stress). Remind students of the confidentiality rule and the time for the next meeting.

What Are My Stressors?

Goals

1. To explain what stressors are and how they affect the stress response
2. To help students identify the people, places, and events that are the biggest stressors in their own lives
3. To promote students' awareness that others in the group have similar stressors and are working to deal with them

Materials

Stressors Rating Scale

Process

Review

1. Review the idea of the stress response, pointing out that changes take place in our bodies when we find ourselves in a threatening situation. Invite students to share their experiences observing their own responses to stressful situations.

Working Time

1. Briefly describe the goals of the session.
2. Explain that *stressors* are the people, places, or events that we respond to with the stress response. Ask students to generate some examples of each type of stressor. Responses might include the following.

    People: The principal, class bully, or coach

    Places: The doctor's office, the basketball court, or the room in which a test will be given

    Events: Hearing that your parents are getting a divorce, getting a test back with a low grade, or having to give a class presentation

3. Explain that stressors can also be thought of in terms of the context in which they occur: school, home, or friendship. Distribute copies of the Stressors Rating Scale and ask students to mark it according to the instructions.
4. After students have had a few minutes to complete the scale, discuss each category of stressor. Encourage them to describe the people, places, or events in each of these contexts that cause them the most stress. Allow plenty of time for comments and feedback.

Closing Time

1. Encourage students to summarize what they have learned about their own stressors. Invite them to explain how it felt for them to talk about their own stressors and to hear about other group members' stressors. Ask whether they would be willing to continue observing their responses to stressful situations outside the group.
2. Ask whether there is anything anyone would like to say before the group ends and mention the topic of the next session (physical, psychological, and behavioral responses to stressors). Remind students of the confidentiality rule and the time for the next meeting.

Name____________________________________ Date________________

Stressors Rating Scale

Instructions: Circle the number that shows how much stress each of the following people, places, or events causes you. Write in any stressors that aren't listed in the spaces marked "other."

Scale 1 = No stress
2 = Slight amount of stress
3 = Moderate amount of stress
4 = A lot of stress
5 = Extremely high stress

School Stressors

1. A particular teacher	1	2	3	4	5
2. Principal	1	2	3	4	5
3. Bully	1	2	3	4	5
4. A certain subject	1	2	3	4	5
5. Feeling less smart than others	1	2	3	4	5
6. Several subjects	1	2	3	4	5
7. Worry about failing	1	2	3	4	5
8. Fear of not getting selected for a team, cheerleading, or other group	1	2	3	4	5
9. Fear of being ridiculed	1	2	3	4	5
10. Fear of not living up to parents' or teachers' expectations	1	2	3	4	5
11. Fear of not getting into a good high school or college	1	2	3	4	5
12. Fear of not knowing what to do after graduation	1	2	3	4	5
13. Other________________	1	2	3	4	5
14. Other________________	1	2	3	4	5
15. Other________________	1	2	3	4	5

Home Stressors

1. Fear of parents' divorcing	1	2	3	4	5
2. Brother's or sister's hurting me	1	2	3	4	5
3. Other family member's hurting me	1	2	3	4	5
4. Fear of parent's remarrying	1	2	3	4	5
5. Not having enough clothes or other supplies	1	2	3	4	5
6. Not getting enough attention	1	2	3	4	5
7. Having so little supervision that it is easy to get in trouble	1	2	3	4	5
8. Not getting enough affection and love	1	2	3	4	5
9. Fighting between parents	1	2	3	4	5
10. Fighting with parents	1	2	3	4	5
11. Illness of family member or self	1	2	3	4	5
12. Having to deal with stepfamily members	1	2	3	4	5
13. Having to move	1	2	3	4	5
14. Other________________	1	2	3	4	5
15. Other________________	1	2	3	4	5

Stressors Rating Scale (cont'd)

Friendship Stressors

1. Losing a friend	1	2	3	4	5
2. Not having enough friends	1	2	3	4	5
3. Having a friend reject me	1	2	3	4	5
4. Having a friend lie to me	1	2	3	4	5
5. Having a friend talk about me behind my back	1	2	3	4	5
6. Feeling unaccepted or disliked	1	2	3	4	5
7. Feeling left out	1	2	3	4	5
8. Having a friend my parents dislike or disapprove of	1	2	3	4	5
9. Worrying about not having a boyfriend or girlfriend	1	2	3	4	5
10. Not knowing how to make friends	1	2	3	4	5
11. Not knowing how to deal with situations involving friends	1	2	3	4	5
12. Not knowing how to stand up for my rights	1	2	3	4	5
13. Feeling unattractive	1	2	3	4	5
14. Other ____________________	1	2	3	4	5
15. Other ____________________	1	2	3	4	5

How I Respond to Stressors

Goals

1. To clarify the physical, psychological, and behavioral effects of stress
2. To help students understand the effects of stress on them as individuals

Materials

Chalkboard or chart paper

Process

Review

1. Encourage students to share their experiences in noticing their own stressors. Did any of them experience something as being a stressor that they hadn't realized previously was stressful? Do any of them think they would like to find ways to reduce the stress associated with these kinds of situations?

Working Time

1. Briefly describe the goals of the session.
2. Explain that being under stress causes three types of effects: physical, psychological, and behavioral. Write the following physical effects on the chalkboard or chart paper.

   - Rapid or pounding heartbeat
   - Dry throat and mouth
   - Feeling excited, keyed up, or nervous
   - Having difficulty speaking
   - Sweating of palms, neck, or other body parts
   - Upset stomach, diarrhea, vomiting
   - Headache
   - Eating too little or too much
   - Problems sleeping

   Encourage students to share the physical signs of stress they themselves experience. Which of the signs do students relate to? What is it like when they feel this way? What would they like to do about these feelings?

3. Describe the following psychological effects of stress. Write these as well on the chalkboard or chart paper.

   - Forgetting things (e.g., the answers to test questions)
   - Feeling emotionally unstable or out of control
   - Feeling depressed or irritable
   - Feeling angry for no apparent reason
   - Getting upset over small things
   - Breaking out into tears easily
   - Accident proneness

   Encourage students to share and discuss the psychological signs of stress they experience.

4. Describe the following behavioral signs of stress, writing them on the chalkboard or chart paper.
    - "Blowing up" in anger
    - Avoiding doing things because of associated stress (e.g., not trying out for a team, club, or activity because of fear of failure)
    - Not admitting you need help
    - Avoiding tough situations
    - Doing hurtful things to other people
    - Arguing with parents
    - Doing things to get in trouble to get attention

    Invite students to share and discuss the behavioral signs of stress they experience.

5. Point out that not every person experiences the same physical, psychological, or behavioral signs of stress: Having any one sign, such as a bad headache, might or might not mean you are under stress. However, having a number of these signs might mean you are not dealing with stress very well.

Closing Time

1. Review the main points in the session. The following discussion questions may help.
    - What did you learn today about how you behave under stress?
    - What did you learn about how stress affects you physically? Psychologically? Behaviorally?
    - Were you surprised about anything you learned today? (Encourage students to observe how stress affects them in these three areas.)

2. Ask whether there is anything anyone would like to say before the group ends and mention the topic of the next session (progressive muscle relaxation training). Instruct students to wear comfortable clothing so they will be able to do the relaxation exercises. Remind students of the confidentiality rule and the time for the next meeting.

Progressive Muscle Relaxation Training

Goals

1. To illustrate progressive muscle relaxation procedures as a potential way of managing stress
2. To give students the opportunity to practice progressive muscle relaxation in the group setting and to encourage them to practice and use the technique outside the group

Materials

Progressive Muscle Relaxation Training Script

Process

Review

1. Invite students to share their experiences in noticing how stress affects them physically, psychologically, and behaviorally. For example, if you are angry, your face might get hot (physical), you might think angry thoughts (psychological), and you might take a walk to help you calm down (behavioral). If you are in love, your heart might pound (physical), you might feel joyful (psychological), and you might smile (behavioral).
2. Ask whether there are any ways students show stress that they would like to change. Discuss.

Working Time

1. Briefly describe the goals of the session.
2. Explain that *progressive muscle relaxation* involves tensing and relaxing your muscles all over your body, one group of muscles at a time, starting with your forehead and progressing through sets of muscles lower and lower in your body. Point out that progressive muscle relaxation works because your muscles only have two ways of being: tense or relaxed. Illustrate these two states by holding your arm limp and then tensing your arm.
3. Challenge students to try to see if the muscles in their arms can be both tense and relaxed at the same time. After it becomes clear that these two states can't exist simultaneously, explain that being able to relax your muscles in a tense situation can help you learn to feel more relaxed all over. Allow everyone in the group to practice tensing and relaxing hand and/or arm muscles. Go around the group to make sure each person knows what is meant by tensing and relaxing.
4. Describe the four steps involved in progressive muscle relaxation.
   - Tense muscles for about 5 seconds.
   - Think about what the muscles feel like when they are tense.
   - Relax the muscles.
   - Think about what the muscles feel like when they are relaxed.
5. Instruct students to move their chairs so that they face the wall. Chairs should be about 4 feet from the wall with plenty of room between them. Read the Progressive Muscle Relaxation Training Script slowly and clearly, instructing students to follow your directions.
6. After the exercise has been completed, have the group move their chairs back into the circle. Discuss the following questions.
   - What did you like about practicing progressive muscle relaxation? What did you dislike?
   - How did you feel when you were doing the exercises?
   - What did you notice about yourself?
   - Do you feel tense or relaxed right now?
   - Do you think doing progressive muscle relaxation again might help you reduce your stress?

Closing Time

1. Distribute copies of the Progressive Muscle Relaxation Training Script. Ask students whether they would be willing to practice progressive muscle relaxation several times between now and the time the group meets again. Encourage them to be specific about when and where they will practice, and whether they will ask someone else to read the script to them or attempt the exercise by themselves.
2. Ask whether there is anything anyone would like to say before the group ends and mention the topic of the next session (thematic imagery). Remind students of the confidentiality rule and the time for the next meeting.

Progressive Muscle Relaxation Training Script

Instructions: When you feel tense, upset, or nervous, certain muscles in your body tighten. By having you deliberately tense certain muscles in your body, you will learn to identify the muscles that are tight; then you learn to relax them. Practice tightening and relaxing the following muscle groups.

Forehead

Wrinkle up your forehead. Point to where it feels particularly tense (over the bridge of the nose and above each eyebrow). Slowly relax your forehead and pay special attention to those areas that are particularly tense. Spend a few seconds noticing how it feels to have those muscles loosen, switch off, and relax. Notice the difference in how the muscles feel.

Eyes

Close your eyes very tightly. Point to where it feels tight. Your eyes should feel tense above and below each eyelid and on the inner and outer edges of the eye. Pay particular attention to those areas that are especially tense. Gradually relax your eyes as you open them slowly. Notice the difference in the way the muscles feel.

Nose

Wrinkle your nose. Point to the areas that feel tight (the bridge and nostrils). Pay special attention to those areas that are particularly tense. Gradually relax your nose slowly, letting all the tension out. Notice how it feels to have those muscles loosen, switch off, then fully relax. Notice the difference in the way the muscles feel.

Smile

Put your mouth and face in a forced smile. Point to the areas that feel tense (the upper and lower lips and cheeks on each side). Your lips should be hard against your cheeks. Gradually relax your face. Notice how it feels to have those muscles loosen, switch off, and relax.

Tongue

Put your tongue hard against the roof of your mouth. Point to where it feels tense (on the inside of the mouth and tongue, and the muscles just below the jaw). Slowly relax those muscles by letting your tongue gradually fall to the floor of your mouth. Pay special attention to those areas that are particularly tense. Notice how it feels to have those muscles loosen, switch off, and relax. Notice the difference in the way the muscles feel.

Jaw

Clench your teeth. Point to where it feels tense (the muscles on the side of your face and also the temples). Gradually relax your jaw and feel the sensation of letting go. Notice how it feels to have those muscles loosen, switch off, and relax. Notice the difference in the way the muscles feel.

Lips

Pucker your lips. Point to where it feels tense (upper and lower lips and side of lips). Pay special attention to those areas that are particularly tense. Gradually relax your lips. Notice how it feels to have those muscles loosen, switch off, and relax. Notice the difference in the way the muscles feel.

Note. From *Relaxation: A Comprehensive Manual for Adults, Children, and Children with Special Needs* (pp. 22–30), by J. R. Cautela and J. Groden, 1978, Champaign, IL: Research Press. Adapted by permission.

Progressive Muscle Relaxation Training Script (cont'd)

Neck

Tighten your neck. Point to where it feels tense (Adam's apple and on each side and the back of the neck). Pay special attention to those areas that are particularly tense. Gradually relax your neck. Notice how it feels to have those muscles loosen, switch off, and relax. Notice the difference in the way the muscles feel.

Arms

Put your right arm out straight, make a fist, and tighten your whole arm from your hand to your shoulder. Point to where it feels tense (biceps, forearm, back of arm, elbow, above and below wrist and fingers). Pay special attention to those areas that are particularly tense. Gradually relax and lower your arm, bending it at the elbow; relax so that your arm is resting on your lap in the relaxing position. Notice how it feels to have those muscles loosen, switch off, and relax. Notice the difference in the way the muscles feel. Repeat with the left arm.

Legs

Now lift your left leg, turn your toes in towards you, and tighten your whole leg. Point to where it feels tight (top and bottom sides of thigh, knee, calf, front and back of arch, and toes). Gradually relax and lower your leg until your foot is squarely on the floor, bending your knee as you relax. Make sure your leg goes back to the relaxing position. Notice the difference in the way the muscles feel. Repeat with the right leg.

Back

Move forward in your chair. Bring your elbows up and try to get them to meet in the back. Notice where it feels particularly tense (shoulders and down the middle of your back). Gradually relax by moving back into the chair while you straighten out your arms and put them on your lap in the relaxing position. Notice how it feels to have those muscles loosen, switch off, and relax.

Chest

Tighten your chest. Try to constrict it or pull it in. Point to where it feels tense (middle of the chest and above and below each breast). Gradually relax your chest. Notice how it feels to have those muscles loosen, switch off, and relax. Notice the difference in the way the muscles feel.

Stomach

Tighten your stomach by pulling it in and making it as hard as a board. Point to where it feels tense (navel and circle around navel encompassing about 4 inches in diameter). Gradually relax your stomach to its natural position. Notice how it feels to have those muscles loosen, switch off, and relax. Notice the difference in the way the muscles feel.

Below the waist

Tighten everything below the waist, including your thighs and your buttocks. You should feel yourself rise from the chair. You may notice that you have to tighten your legs a bit. Notice where it is particularly tense (top, bottom, and sides of thighs; muscles from the rear that make contact with the chair). Gradually relax and move back in your chair. Notice the difference in the way the muscles feel.

Thematic Imagery

Goals

1. To illustrate the use of thematic imagery as a potential way of managing stress
2. To give students the opportunity to practice thematic imagery in the group setting and to encourage them to practice and use the technique outside the group

Materials

Thematic Imagery Script

Process

Review

1. Invite students to share their experiences using progressive muscle relaxation on their own. Did using this technique help them reduce stress? If not, do they think the technique might be worth trying again?

Working Time

1. Briefly describe the goals of the session.
2. Explain that *thematic imagery* involves picturing relaxing situations and that using this technique is another way of reducing stress. Because this method is entirely mental, it might be easier to do at certain times than progressive muscle relaxation.
3. Guide students by reading the Thematic Imagery Script in a slow, calm voice.
4. Discuss students' experiences, using the following questions.
   - How did it feel to be floating away to a wonderful place in your imagination?
   - What was your special place? Did everyone visualize the same place?
   - How do you think this technique could help you deal with stress?
   - Do you think this technique would work as well as progressive muscle relaxation? Why or why not?
   - In what situations do you think thematic imagery would be useful?
5. Point out that students have absolute freedom in whatever images they choose and that a "self-guided" and shortened version of the exercise illustrated in the group can be helpful in any number of stressful situations: before taking a test, going to the dentist, asking someone for a date, giving a speech, and so forth. It is important to stress, however, that this technique is more effective for some people than for others. People who have trouble vividly imagining a scene might prefer progressive muscle relaxation or another stress reduction technique.

Closing Time

1. Ask students whether they would be willing to try thematic imagery in addition to progressive muscle relaxation to help them manage their stress. Distribute copies of the Thematic Imagery Script and discuss the specific situations in which students think they will be able to use the technique.
2. Ask whether there is anything anyone would like to say before the group ends and mention the topic of the next session (using positive coping statements). Remind students of the confidentiality rule and the time for the next meeting.

Thematic Imagery Script

Instructions: In this exercise we are going to relax by letting our minds dwell on a relaxing scene or setting.

PAUSE

Make sure you are in a comfortable position.

PAUSE

Are your feet flat on the floor?

PAUSE

Are your hands resting comfortably in your lap?

PAUSE

Now gently close your eyes and let yourself settle into a position that is comfortable.

PAUSE

For the next minute or so, your body becomes more and more quiet.

PAUSE 1 MINUTE

Let yourself begin to settle down and relax as you remain still.

PAUSE

Now attend to your body.

PAUSE

Let your breathing be calm and even.

PAUSE

Let every outgoing breath carry away any tension you might feel.

PAUSE

Let yourself feel more and more comfortably relaxed.

PAUSE

And now quietly ask yourself, "What scene or setting is most relaxing to me at the moment?"

PAUSE 10 SECONDS

You might want to picture a quiet beach, or a grassy plain, or a cool mountain top, or a peaceful pond. Whatever scene or setting is most relaxing to you, let it come to you in whatever way it wishes.

PAUSE 10 SECONDS

And now, quietly let your mind dwell on this scene for the next few seconds.

PAUSE 15 SECONDS

Let the scene become as vivid and real as possible.

Note. From *Relaxation Dynamics: A Cognitive-Behavioral Approach to Relaxation* (pp. 167–169), by J. C. Smith, 1989, Champaign, IL: Research Press. Reprinted by permission.

PAUSE 10 SECONDS

How does it look?

PAUSE 10 SECONDS

Can you see the sky?

PAUSE

Can you feel the wind brushing against your skin?

PAUSE

Can you smell the gentle, cool air?

PAUSE

Can you feel the warm sunlight or perhaps the cool night air?

PAUSE

Involve all your senses.

PAUSE

What do you see?

PAUSE

What do you hear?

PAUSE

What is touching your skin?

PAUSE

Can you taste or smell anything?

PAUSE

And let the scene grow in whatever way is most relaxing to you.

PAUSE 10 SECONDS

Perhaps words come to your mind that describe the scene.

PAUSE

If words or phrases come, simply let them repeat over and over like echoes.

PAUSE

Try not to force these words to change or make sense. Simply let them repeat over and over, very peacefully and quietly.

PAUSE

There is nothing for you to do except to attend quietly to your relaxing scene.

PAUSE

Let it change and evolve on its own.

PAUSE 15 SECONDS

If you find yourself engaged in thinking about something or trying to figure something out, that's OK.

PAUSE

Quietly and gently return to your relaxing scene.

PAUSE 15 SECONDS

Let yourself sink deeper and deeper into a pleasant state of relaxation.

PAUSE

From time to time, let yourself quietly repeat whatever words or pictures suggest deeper, more complete, and more satisfying relaxation.

PAUSE

You might think the words "I am sinking deeper and deeper" or "I am letting go more and more" or "There is nothing for me to do but let go" or "I am more fully aware."

PAUSE

Let the deepening suggestions come to you in whatever way feels most satisfying and relaxing.

PAUSE 10 SECONDS

Again and again, every time your mind wanders or is distracted, return to your pleasant, relaxing scene.

PAUSE

Continue attending to your scene for the next few minutes. See where it leads you. See how it deepens. See how it grows and becomes more relaxing.

PAUSE 2 MINUTES

And now, very gently let go of what you are attending to.

PAUSE 5 SECONDS

When you are ready, gently open your eyes.

PAUSE 5 SECONDS

Take a deep breath.

PAUSE 5 SECONDS

And stretch.

PAUSE 5 SECONDS

This completes the thematic imagery exercise.

Positive Coping Statements

Goals

1. To introduce students to the stress inoculation technique of using positive coping statements [2]
2. To give students practice in making positive coping statements inside and outside of the group

Materials

Positive Coping Statements Worksheet
Index cards

Process

Review

1. Discuss students' experiences in using thematic imagery to help manage stress. In what situations did they use the technique? What was the outcome? Do they think they will continue using thematic imagery? How was using this technique different from using progressive muscle relaxation?

Working Time

1. Briefly describe the goals of the session.
2. Ask whether any students have gone to the doctor to get an inoculation (shot) to prevent mumps, chicken pox, measles, or any other disease. (Groans and head shakes.) Why do they think they got these shots? Do they always work? What about flu shots? Do they work most of the time?
3. Explain that *stress inoculation* is a technique that helps people face stressful situations that can't be avoided, like taking a big test or going to the dentist. Point out that, like being vaccinated against a disease, using stress inoculation techniques can prevent you from having stress or keep you from suffering as much as you might. Part of stress inoculation involves making *positive coping statements* before, during, and after a stressful situation.
4. Discuss the fact that when we know a situation is going to be unpleasant, we often tell ourselves how awful or terrible it is going to be. As a result, we may actually cause the situation to be just as bad as we think it will be. Invite students to name some stressful and unavoidable situations they have experienced. From those generated, choose one situation to illustrate the use of positive coping statements. For example: Giving a 5-minute report on the USSR in class next Friday.

   Positive coping statements before the situation

   - I've read a lot about the USSR—I can share my knowledge with the class.
   - It's only a 5-minute report, not 30 minutes.
   - I don't have to go first, so I can model my report after the good ones that come before it.
   - I did this OK last year.
   - I'm not going to say negative things to myself.
   - I'm going to be OK.
   - I can deal with this!
   - It's OK to be nervous.

[2] The guidelines presented here are based on the work of Donald Meichenbaum in *Stress-inoculation Training*, 1985, Elmsford, NY: Pergamon.

Positive coping statements during the situation

- I'm doing my best—that's all anyone can ask.
- I can handle this.
- Take three deep breaths and try to relax.
- It will be over in a minute.
- Just relax.
- One step at a time.
- I can always look at my notes.
- I really want to share this idea with my classmates.

Positive coping statements after the situation

- I did it!
- I did a good job.
- I can relax now—it's over.
- I handled the situation pretty well.
- I'm proud of myself!
- I can deal with tough situations.
- I can hardly wait to tell ________ about how I did.
- I can do this again in the future and succeed.

5. Distribute copies of the Positive Coping Statements Worksheet and instruct students to write down a stressful situation they think they will face in the near future. (These situations don't necessarily have to be major ones—minor stressors will work just as well.)
6. After giving students a few minutes to write down a situation, ask them to take turns sharing their situations with the group. The group is to brainstorm coping statements that could be used before, during, and after each situation.
7. Have students copy their statements from the Positive Coping Statements Worksheet onto index cards they can carry with them to help remind them of what they want to say to themselves.

Closing Time

1. Invite students to practice making positive coping statements in stressful situations outside the group. Encourage them to talk about what they think might happen if they use positive coping statements and how they feel about trying this technique. Remind them that they can also use the skills they learned for progressive muscle relaxation and thematic imagery.
2. Ask whether there is anything anyone would like to say before the group ends and mention the topic of the next session (practicing positive coping statements). Remind students of the confidentiality rule and the time for the next meeting.

Name____ Date__________________

Positive Coping Statements Worksheet

Instructions: Write down a stressful situation you think you may face in the near future. Then think of several coping statements you could use before, during, and after the situation.

Situation____

____

____

____

Statements before the situation

1. ____
2. ____
3. ____
4. ____
5. ____

Statements during the situation

1. ____
2. ____
3. ____
4. ____
5. ____

Statements after the situation

1. ____
2. ____
3. ____
4. ____
5. ____

Practicing Positive Coping Statements

Goals

1. To provide additional practice in generating positive coping statements by using the self-as-model technique [3]

Materials

Two or three tape recorders and blank audiotapes as needed

Positive Coping Statements Worksheet (from Session 6)

Process

Review

1. Invite students to share their experiences in using positive coping statements to "inoculate" themselves against stress. The following discussion questions may be helpful.
   - What stressful situations did you face since the last group session?
   - Did you use your positive coping statements? Did they help you to reduce your level of stress?
   - What was using positive coping statements like for you?
   - If the technique didn't work for you, are you willing to try it a few more times before giving up?

Working Time

1. Briefly describe the goals of the session.
2. Ask for a volunteer to read the statements listed on his or her Positive Coping Statements Worksheet into the tape recorder. Explain that recording the statements in your own voice can help you feel more comfortable using them and that practicing can make it easier for you to make up coping statements for unexpected stressful situations (e.g., a pop quiz).
3. Have the volunteer record the coping statements, then play them back for the group. Encourage discussion about what hearing the statements read aloud is like.
4. Go through the same procedure with the other group members, allowing them to record their statements as many times as they wish until they feel comfortable with their performance. Depending on the time and equipment available (as well as the maturity of group members), you may have students pair up and practice recording their statements with each other. If time is short, you can offer to help members record their statements later.
5. After students have had a chance to record their statements, discuss the following questions.
   - What do you think of the idea of recording your positive coping statements and listening to yourself repeat them?
   - How do you think this kind of practice could help you deal with stressful situations?
   - If you don't have a tape recorder, what other ways can you think of to practice making positive coping statements?

---

[3] For further information on this technique, see W. H. Cormier and L. S. Cormier, *Interviewing Strategies for Helpers*, 1985, Monterey, CA: Brooks/Cole; and R. Hosford, *Counseling Techniques* (Self-as-Model Film), 1974, Washington, DC: Personnel and Guidance Press.

Closing Time

1. Encourage students to continue using positive coping statements to help them deal with the stressful situations they face. Remind them that they can also continue to use the skills they learned for progressive muscle relaxation and thematic imagery.
2. Ask whether there is anything anyone would like to say before the group ends and mention the topic of the final session (reviewing what has been learned in the group and saying goodbye). Remind students of the confidentiality rule and the time for the next meeting.

Saying Goodbye

Goals

1. To provide a review of what has happened in the past seven sessions
2. To help students understand and cope with the stress involved in having the group end
3. To illustrate the importance of saying goodbye and give students a chance to achieve closure on the group and their relationships in it

Materials

Nutritious snack for everyone (raisins, fruit drink, etc.)

Process

Review

1. Invite students to share their experiences since the last session in dealing with stressful situations. Praise them for their attempts thus far and encourage them to keep using progressive muscle relaxation, thematic imagery, and positive coping statements.
2. Next, go through the session topics and discuss what students feel are the most important lessons they learned in the group. The following questions may be helpful.
   - What is meant by the *stress response?* How has our stress response changed since prehistoric times? (Session 1)
   - What things are the biggest stressors for you? (Session 2)
   - In what three areas does stress affect us? *(physical, psychological, behavioral)* Which of these effects do you notice when you are under stress? (Session 3)
   - Is progressive muscle relaxation a good way for you to reduce stress? Why or why not? (Session 4)
   - In what situations have you used thematic imagery? Do you think this technique has helped you reduce your stress? (Session 5)
   - What is meant by *stress inoculation?* What is one way you can "inoculate" yourself against stress? *(positive coping statements)* Has using positive coping statements been helpful to you? Why or why not? (Sessions 6 and 7)

Working Time

1. Point out that one source of stress is change and that having the group end may be a stressful situation for some members. Encourage students to talk about ways they might cope with this change.
2. Discuss the importance of goodbyes, stressing that saying goodbye can help people deal with sadness when a relationship ends and go on to new relationships.
3. Invite students to say goodbye by making a positive, affirming statement to each person in the group. Begin this process by modeling the statements yourself. For example, "Randy, you worked very hard in the group, and I think you will be able to handle your stress better in the future" or "Janine, I certainly appreciated your willingness to share your personal experiences with us."

Closing Time

1. Thank students for participating and remind them of the confidentiality rule. Tell students that, even though the group is ending, you will continue to be available to them (if indeed this is the case) and that you hope the friendships made in the group will continue.
2. Encourage members to have a "group hug" if the atmosphere seems right, then share the snacks.

Better Ways of Getting Mad: Anger Management Skills

Anger is one of our primary emotions. Unfortunately, it is one that is frequently dealt with inappropriately. Many people learn unhealthy ways of processing anger, from suppressing and repressing angry feelings to exploding in rage with little provocation. Because adults frequently do not model appropriate ways to process anger, young adolescents sometimes do not have the opportunity to learn these skills, and their responses are inappropriate and ineffective.

A significant body of research evidence suggests that inappropriate anger responses can be replaced with more appropriate and effective behavior (Abikoff, 1979; Bender, 1976; Camp, Blom, Hebert, & Van Doornick, 1977; Cormier & Cormier, 1985; Ellis & Bernard, 1984; Kendall & Braswell, 1981). Some of the research-supported techniques that have been used to help youth manage anger responses are self-instruction (Novaco, 1975; Snyder & White, 1977), problem-solving training (Douglas, 1975; Spivack, Platt, & Shure, 1976), self-control training (Allen, Chinsky, Larcen, Lochman, & Selinger, 1976), cognitive restructuring (Forman, 1980), stress inoculation (Feindler & Fremouw, 1983), and rational-emotive therapy (Morris & Kanitz, 1975).

Although many different techniques can be used to help youngsters learn and practice anger management skills, most are based on a three-step process: (1) becoming aware of behaviors that are hurtful to self and/or others; (2) learning skills or techniques to replace hurtful behaviors; and (3) practicing until the new, more adaptive behaviors become usable in real-life situations. By having these new behaviors in their repertoires, young adolescents can better function in school, at home, and with peers.

Group Objectives

1. To explore the origins of anger and illustrate that anger as an emotion is neither good nor bad
2. To help students become aware of situational, physical, and cognitive clues that precede angry responses and identify their own typical patterns of response in anger-provoking situations
3. To distinguish between appropriate and inappropriate anger responses and help students see that appropriate responses generally have more positive consequences
4. To present the use of coping statements and cognitive restructuring as positive means of reducing angry feelings
5. To encourage students to take personal responsibility for their own thoughts, feelings, and behaviors

Selection and Other Guidelines

The following target signs may indicate that a student is a candidate for this particular group experience.

1. Being easily influenced by peers
2. Low tolerance for frustration (i.e., a "short fuse")
3. Inability to deal with figures of authority
4. Poor verbal control of overt behaviors
5. Poor self-control for this age group (i.e., the inability to think before acting)
6. Lack of understanding reasons for angry feelings or options for expressing anger

In addition to following the general selection guidelines outlined in the Introduction, choose students with heterogeneous skills in expressing anger. A good mix would include one or two students each who express their anger in the following ways: (1) fighting or bullying other students; (2) having problems with authority figures rather than peers; (3) directing their feelings inward and behaving passively; (4) engaging in self-defeating or self-destructive behaviors (e.g., refusing to study, avoiding responsibility); and (5) avoiding provocative social situations because they lack the self-confidence to deal with their anger. Your colleagues may pressure you to select only those students who act out the most because they present the greatest problem to others. However, because appropriate role models are especially important in this group, you should take special care to balance your group to include students who already possess some positive skills. Many angry youngsters have experienced a great deal of punishment from adults and may be unsure about what will be happening in group. Use the early sessions to develop a feeling of safety in members.

It is also important to point out that students may have learned and practiced inappropriate anger responses over their lifespans and that change may be difficult and painful. Some youths may not be able to exhibit enough self-control to cooperate in a group; for them, individual counseling may be more effective.

References and Recommended Reading

Abikoff, H. (1979). Cognitive training interventions in children: Review of a new approach. *Journal of Learning Disabilities, 12,* 65–77.

Allen, G., Chinsky, J., Larcen, S., Lochman, J., & Selinger, W. (1976). *Community psychology and the schools: A behaviorally oriented multi-level preventive approach.* Hillsdale, NJ: Erlbaum.

Bender, N. (1976). Self-verbalization versus tutor verbalization in modifying impulsivity. *Journal of Educational Psychology, 68,* 347–354.

Camp, E., Blom, G., Hebert, F., & Van Doornick, W. (1977). "Think aloud": A program for developing self-control in young aggressive boys. *Journal of Abnormal Child Psychology, 8,* 157–169.

Cormier, W. H., & Cormier, L. S. (1985). *Interviewing strategies for helpers* (2nd ed.). Monterey, CA: Brooks/Cole.

Douglas, V. (1975). Are drugs enough? To treat or to train the hyperactive child. *International Journal of Mental Health, 5,* 199–212.

Ellis, A. (1977). *Anger: How to live with it and without it.* Secaucus, NJ: Citadel.

Ellis, A., & Bernard, M. E. (1984). *Rational-emotive approaches to the problems of childhood.* New York: Plenum.

Feindler, E. L., & Fremouw, W. J. (1983). Stress inoculation training for adolescent anger problems. In D. H. Meichenbaum & M. E. Jaremko (Eds.), *Stress reduction and prevention.* New York: Plenum.

Forman, S. G. (1980). A comparison of cognitive training and response cost procedures in modifying aggressive behavior of elementary school children. *Behavior Therapy, 11,* 594–600.

Goldstein, A. P., & Glick, B. (1987). *Aggression replacement training: A comprehensive intervention for aggressive youth.* Champaign, IL: Research Press.

Kendall, P., & Braswell, L. (1984). *Cognitive-behavioral intervention with impulsive children.* New York: Guilford.

Meichenbaum, D., & Cameron, R. (1983). Stress inoculation training: Toward a general paradigm for training coping skills. In D. H. Meichenbaum & M. E. Jaremko (Eds.), *Stress reduction and prevention.* New York: Plenum.

Meyers, A. W., & Craighead, W. E. (1984). *Cognitive behavior therapy with children.* New York: Plenum.

Morris, K. T., & Kanitz, H. M. (1975). *Rational-emotive therapy.* Boston: Houghton Mifflin.

Novaco, R. W. (1975). *Anger control: The development and evaluation of an experimental treatment.* Lexington, MA: Heath.

Schneider, M., & Robin, A. (1976). The turtle technique: A method for the self-control of impulsive behavior. In J. Krumboltz & C. Thoresen (Eds.), *Counseling methods.* New York: Holt, Rinehart & Winston.

Snyder, J., & White, M. (1977). *The use of cognitive self-instruction in the treatment of behaviorally disturbed adolescents.* Unpublished manuscript, Wichita State University, Kansas.

Spivack, G., Platt, J., & Shure, M. (1976). *The problem-solving approach to adjustment.* San Francisco: Jossey-Bass.

Walen, S. R., DiGiuseppe, R., & Wessler, R. L. (1980). *A practitioner's guide to rational-emotive therapy.* New York: Oxford University Press.

Getting Started

Goals

1. To help students become acquainted and feel comfortable in the group setting
2. To choose appropriate ground rules for the group sessions
3. To identify why students want to be a part of the group and what they hope to learn
4. To explore the origins of anger and point out that the emotion of anger is neither good nor bad

Materials

An old record album or cassette tape
Anger Situations Form
Writing paper
Chalkboard or chart paper

Process

Ice Breaker

1. Welcome students and briefly describe the goals of the group in general as well as this session in particular.
2. Hold up the record album or cassette tape and explain that one side represents the way students are now and that the other side represents the way they would like to be in the future.
3. Distribute the writing paper and instruct students to "record" on one side of the paper three positive things about themselves that are true now and that they would be willing to share with the group. Suggest a number of statements reflecting different attributes (physical, social, intellectual, etc.). For example:
   - I'm a pretty good football player.
   - I have nice eyes.
   - I can admit when I'm wrong.
   - I ride my horse in shows and win some ribbons.
   - I make my friends laugh.
4. When students have finished, instruct them to turn their papers over and write three positive things they would like to be true in the future. For example:
   - I'd like to be a better big brother.
   - I'd like to be able to get along with teachers.
   - I'd like to know what I'm going to be when I get out of school.
   - I'd like to be taller.
   - I'd like to stop getting in so many fights.
5. Invite students to pair up and share the following information with their partners: name, positive present and future attributes, and what they hope to learn from the group. Let students know that they will be introducing their partners to the group after they have shared this information.
6. After a few minutes, reassemble as a group. Model the introductions by sharing the information about yourself first. For example: "My name is Mr. Art Anderson. I play a pretty good game of racquetball, am good with numbers, and think I'm a pretty sharp dresser. In the future, I'd like to own a new car, learn to sing better, and spend more time with my family. I hope to learn all about you and help you deal with your anger better." Ask for volunteers to share the information they learned about their partners in similar fashion until everyone has been introduced.

Working Time

1. Introduce the idea of ground rules, pointing out that rules help everyone be respected and have time to talk. Suggest a few basic ground rules, such as the following.
   - What we say and do here is private and stays in the group (confidentiality rule).
   - Everyone has the right to "pass"—that is, not to participate in an activity or part of an activity.
   - No fighting or arguing.
   - Each person gets time to talk.
   - When someone is talking, everyone else will listen.
2. Ask students to think of other ground rules for the group. List all rules on the chalkboard or on chart paper.
3. Next, bring up the topic of anger, explaining that anger is a very basic human emotion and is neither good nor bad: Even babies and young children express anger when they are tired, cold, hungry, or frustrated. Anger can even have a protective function, as when a dog growls and bites to protect its bone or when we respond angrily when someone abuses our rights, treats us disrespectfully, or takes something from us.
4. Explain that, although anger itself is neutral, the ways we have learned to express our anger can be either *appropriate* (helpful to us and those around us) or *inappropriate* (hurtful to ourselves and others). If we want to learn more appropriate ways to express our anger, we must first recognize what kind of situations we respond to with anger. (Avoid saying that situations and people *cause* our anger or *make* us angry because such language is in conflict with the important idea that people are responsible for their own feelings and behavior.)

Closing Time

1. Distribute copies of the Anger Situations Form and explain that the vertical column on the form shows different situations that might set students up for an angry response and the horizontal row lists people with whom students might become angry. Ask whether students would be willing to put a checkmark in the appropriate box when they find themselves becoming angry with someone or something. Illustrate the use of the form, if necessary, and encourage students to mark the form daily so they won't forget any incidents.
2. Share a positive statement about each group member and thank each one for coming. For example: "Susie, you shared some personal things today. Thank you for trusting us so much" or "Bob, I appreciated your idea for a ground rule. I'm glad you'll be a part of the group."
3. Ask whether there is anything anyone would like to say before the group ends and mention the topic of the next session (recognizing anger clues). Remind students of the confidentiality rule and the time for the next meeting.

Name________________________________ Date________________

Anger Situations Form

Instructions: Put a checkmark in the appropriate box to show the people and situations that are involved in your anger.

	People							
Situations	Mom	Dad	Sister	Brother	Friend	Teacher	Other	Other
Not getting what I want	☐	☐	☐	☐	☐	☐	☐	☐
Unfair treatment	☐	☐	☐	☐	☐	☐	☐	☐
Loss (friendship, opportunity, etc.)	☐	☐	☐	☐	☐	☐	☐	☐
Fights	☐	☐	☐	☐	☐	☐	☐	☐
Disrespect	☐	☐	☐	☐	☐	☐	☐	☐
Dishonesty	☐	☐	☐	☐	☐	☐	☐	☐
Other	☐	☐	☐	☐	☐	☐	☐	☐
Other	☐	☐	☐	☐	☐	☐	☐	☐

Recognizing Anger Clues

Goals

1. To promote awareness of situational, cognitive, and physical clues that may precede an angry response
2. To help students identify their own typical patterns of response when angry

Materials

Anger Situations Form (self-improvement exercise from Session 1)

Process

Review

1. Invite students to share information from their completed Anger Situations Forms. The following discussion questions may be helpful.
   - What was it like for you to keep track of the people and situations that seem to provoke your anger?
   - Are you able to identify which situations cause you the most trouble? What are some of them?
   - Who are the people with whom you get the most angry?
2. Instruct students to keep their Anger Situations Forms for use at a later time (Session 5).

Working Time

1. Briefly describe the goals of the session.
2. Discuss the fact that anger doesn't happen instantaneously. First, there is frequently a *trigger,* like the situations students noted on their Anger Situations Forms. Often, this trigger situation is accompanied by a number of other clues that show when a person may be on the brink of an angry response. Sometimes, when you see or hear these clues, you can get mad before the situation even happens. For example, if you frequently get into trouble in a certain class, you may feel angry just thinking about being there.
3. Point out that these clues can be either *situational* (in the situation), *cognitive* (in your mind), or *physical* (in your body). Encourage students to play "detective" and try to identify and classify several of the clues they think could precede an angry response. For example:
   - Someone makes an obscene gesture at you. *(situational)*
   - You see someone coming down the hall you don't like. *(situational)*
   - Your face gets hot and your fists clench. *(physical)*
   - You've broken a rule and think your parents might yell at you. *(cognitive)*
   - Your heart starts pounding. *(physical)*
   - You start remembering how someone talked about you behind your back. *(cognitive)*
4. Invite students to share which anger clues they have noticed in themselves and how they generally respond when they are angry. The following discussion questions may be helpful.
   - What kinds of things do you do when you get angry?
   - Which of these clues have you noticed before? Do you think you will notice more of them after today's session?
   - How do you think being aware of these clues could help you in the future?

5. Help students brainstorm ways they might avoid making an angry response. Ideas might include the following.
   - *Ignore the situation or person.* You could leave the situation or not respond to the person at all.
   - *Consider the consequences.* You could ask yourself what your angry response will cost you and then decide what is in your own best interests.
   - *Take five deep breaths or count to 10.* You could take deep breaths or count to 10 silently to give yourself a chance to relax and cool down. After this, you may not feel you need to react as strongly.
   - *Make calming self-statements.* You could say things to yourself like "I'm in control of myself here," "I'm not going to let this get to me," or "I can deal with this situation."

   Let students know you will be looking in more detail into ways to avoid angry responses in future sessions.

Closing Time

1. Invite students to be detectives and look for the clues that will let them know in advance that they may need to take some steps to control their typical anger responses. Ask them which clues they intend to look for and which of the techniques discussed they think would work best for them.
2. Ask whether there is anything anyone would like to say before the group ends and mention the topic of the next session (understanding the difference between appropriate and inappropriate expressions of anger). Remind students of the confidentiality rule and the time for the next meeting.

Appropriate or Inappropriate?

Goals

1. To help students distinguish between appropriate and inappropriate responses to anger
2. To provide students with an appropriate way of stating angry feelings
3. To illustrate that inappropriate angry responses are often also ineffective ones

Materials

Sample Anger Log
Anger Log

Process

Review

1. Discuss what students learned by noticing their own anger clues. Were they able to be detectives and pick up clues to situations that would get them into trouble? What clues did they notice? Did they make any changes in their behavior because they recognized a clue?

Working Time

1. Briefly describe the goals of the session.
2. Review the idea that because anger is a basic emotion, it is neither good nor bad—it just is. Stress once again that, although the feeling of anger is neutral, how we act when angry can be either *appropriate* or *inappropriate.*
3. Invite students to generate a list of some ways people behave when angry that they think are inappropriate or hurtful to that person or others. Examples might include screaming or cursing at someone, hurting someone physically, or lying or cheating to get revenge. Another inappropriate way of expressing anger is to turn the emotion inward—to hurt yourself or to become depressed.
4. Next, ask students to list ways they feel are appropriate to express anger. Elicit the idea that if your anger is justified, it is OK to say how you feel in an honest, straightforward way. One way of doing this is to use an *I message.* Offer several examples of how you could use such messages to express your angry feelings without attacking someone else. For example:
   - "I feel angry when you say you will call at a certain time and then you don't" *not* "You jerk, you never call when you say you will!"
   - "I'm upset that you gave me a bad grade on my report. What should I have done to do better?" *not* "Teachers are all unfair—and you're the worst!"
5. Ask students to generate appropriate *I messages* for several difficult situations: being bullied, being grounded by your parents, having your brother break your new cassette tape, and so forth. Point out that what these statements have in common is that you take responsibility for your own angry feelings and avoid blaming others.
6. Ask students to identify what they think the consequences are of expressing anger appropriately versus inappropriately in several of the situations discussed. For example, if you get a bad grade and say, "Teachers are all unfair—and you're the worst!" your teacher will be less likely to change your grade than if you ask what you could have done better and discuss the situation calmly. In other words, expressing anger appropriately is often in your own best interests.

Closing Time

1. Distribute several copies of the Anger Log to each student. Ask whether students would be willing to use these logs to record how they are feeling and to help them choose how they will respond each time they find themselves in an anger-provoking situation. (Make additional copies of the Anger Log available to students on an as-needed basis during following sessions.) Sharing the Sample Anger Log will help students understand what is expected of them.
2. Ask whether there is anything anyone would like to say before the group ends and mention the topic of the next session (using coping statements for anger control). Remind students of the confidentiality rule and the time for the next meeting.

Name *Bob G.* Date *4/13/90*

Sample Anger Log

Instructions: Fill out this log each time you find yourself in an anger-provoking situation.

1. What is the situation? Who is involved?

   My math teacher tore up my homework because he said it was "sloppy."

2. On a scale of 1–5, how angry am I?

   1 irritated

   2 ticked off

   3 upset

   ④ extremely angry

   5 major blow up

3. What will I say or do to respond?

   I'll walk out of the class.

4. Is this response appropriate ☐ or inappropriate ☒? Why?

   He'll be mad at me for walking out.

5. What will the consequences of my response probably be? Will I end up getting what I want?

   He will still give me the bad grade. I will still be mad and will hate math even more.

Name______________________________ Date______________

Anger Log

Instructions: Fill out this log each time you find yourself in an anger-provoking situation.

1. What is the situation? Who is involved?

2. On a scale of 1–5, how angry am I?

   1 irritated

   2 ticked off

   3 upset

   4 extremely angry

   5 major blow up

3. What will I say or do to respond?

4. Is this response appropriate ☐ or inappropriate ☐? Why?

5. What will the consequences of my response probably be? Will I end up getting what I want?

Coping Statements for Anger Control

Goals

1. To illustrate that what we tell ourselves about situations (*self-talk*) influences how we feel in that situation [1]
2. To give students practice in using coping statements to help control their anger
3. To encourage students to use coping statements in appropriate situations outside the group

Materials

Anger Log (self-improvement exercise from Session 3)
Coping Statements Handout
Anger Control Role Plays

Process

Review

1. Invite students to discuss what they learned from keeping the Anger Log. The following questions may be helpful.
   - In what situations did you find yourself feeling angry?
   - How angry did you get in these situations? A little bit? A lot?
   - What happened to your angry feelings after you stopped to fill out an Anger Log?
   - Were you able to respond appropriately by using an *I message* in all of the situations in which you were angry? If not, what do you think kept you from acting appropriately?
   - Did thinking of the consequences of your response affect what you finally chose to do?
   - Did you notice any connection between the kind of response you made (appropriate or inappropriate) and getting what you wanted?

Working Time

1. Briefly describe the goals of the session.
2. Explain that one way of reducing inappropriate anger responses is to use *coping statements.* Coping statements are positive, helpful things you tell yourself that replace the negative, hurtful things you tell yourself.
3. Distribute copies of the Coping Statements Handout. Ask students whether they think saying these positive things to themselves would have any impact on their angry feelings about a situation. Tell students you will be conducting an experiment to see whether or not coping statements might be helpful in reducing angry feelings.
4. Ask students to pair up, then give each pair a copy of the Anger Control Role Plays. Tell students that you want them to discuss the situations on the list and that when the group reassembles you will be asking for volunteers to act out the scenes.
5. Reassemble the group and invite pairs to conduct the role plays, first without coping statements, then with them. Encourage other group members to suggest additional coping statements if the role players get "stuck." After each role play, ask the following questions.

---

[1] The ideas and example coping statements in this session are based on the work of R. W. Novaco in *Anger Control: The Development and Evaluation of an Experimental Treatment,* 1975, Lexington, MA: Heath.

To the players

- How did it feel to act out this scene in front of the group?
- Have you ever been in a situation like this? What did you do?
- Did using the coping statements help you control your anger?
- What do you think might have happened next if you hadn't used coping statements?

To the group

- Have you ever been in a situation like this? What did you do?
- Was it easy or difficult to think of coping statements the role players could use?
- Do you think you could use coping statements in a real-life situation?

6. Point out that the coping statements students practiced in the role plays were helpful during the situation, but that these kinds of statements can also be used before a situation arises and after a situation is over. Guide students in brainstorming some examples.

   Before a situation

   - This is going to upset me, but I know how to deal with it.
   - I can work out a plan to handle this.
   - Easy does it. Remember to stay relaxed.
   - Try not to take this too seriously.
   - I've done OK in situations like this before.

   After a situation

   - Forget about it. Thinking about it will only make you more upset.
   - I'll get better at this as I go along.
   - Can you laugh it off? It's probably not so serious.
   - That wasn't as bad as I thought.
   - I handled that situation pretty well.

Closing Time

1. Ask students what they learned about using coping statements. Do they think they would be willing to try using this technique between now and the next group? What kinds of situations do they anticipate? Encourage them to continue recording responses on their Anger Logs.
2. Ask whether there is anything anyone would like to say before the group ends and mention the topic of the next session (the ABC's of anger). Remind students of the confidentiality rule and the time for the next meeting.

Coping Statements Handout

Instructions: Try using some of these statements the next time you feel yourself getting angry. Make up your own!

1. Stay calm. Just relax.
2. As long as I keep my cool, I'm in control.
3. Just roll with the punches; don't get bent out of shape.
4. Think of what you want to get out of this.
5. You don't need to prove yourself to anyone.
6. There's no point in getting mad.
7. Look for the positives.
8. I'm not going to let this get to me.
9. It's really a shame she has to act like this.
10. He's probably really unhappy if he's acting that irritable.
11. What she says doesn't matter.
12. I can't expect people to act the way I want them to all the time.
13. My muscles feel tight. Time to relax.
14. She'd probably like me to fly off the handle. Well, she's going to be disappointed.
15. Let's work this problem out. Maybe he has a point.
16. I'm not going to be pushed around, but I'm not going to lose it either.
17. I'm under control. I can handle this.
18. I have a right to be annoyed, but let's try to reason this out.
19. Slow down. Take a few deep breaths.
20. Try to reason it out. Treat each other with respect.

Anger Control Role Plays

Instructions: Read over the situations below, then decide what coping statements you might use to help you deal with each.

Situation 1

Student #1: Let me copy your homework. If you don't let me copy it, I'll tell Ms. Smith you copied yours from Dan O'Brien.

Student #2: Feels very upset and tries to decide whether or not to give homework.

Situation 2

Coach: *(to student)* Gonzales, I want you to go out there and hit that ball over the fence, or you can get off the team right now.

Gonzales: Becomes angry and can hardly walk to the plate without crying.

Situation 3

Parent: *(to child)* You can't go to the show. You have to clean your room completely, including the closets.

Child: Feels furious because parent previously gave permission to go.

Situation 4

Principal: *(to student)* You'll have to stay after school every night for 2 weeks for smoking in the bathroom.

Student: Becomes angry because other student caught smoking gets away with it without any punishment.

Situation 5

Student: *(to teacher)* You pick on me because I'm black. No one else in here got a *D* on the social studies project.

Teacher: Feels frustrated because student really did do poor work.

The ABC's of Anger

Goals

1. To allow students to share information about how they respond in anger-provoking situations
2. To introduce the idea that situations do not cause feelings but that thoughts about situations cause feelings [2]
3. To encourage students to substitute more moderate thoughts in order to control their angry feelings

Materials

Anger Log (self-improvement exercise from Session 4)

Anger Situations Form (self-improvement exercise from Session 1)

Chalkboard or chart paper

Process

Review

1. Invite students to share their experiences in using coping statements. Did using these statements help them to control their angry feelings? What situations did they record on their Anger Logs?

Working Time

1. Briefly describe the goals of the session.
2. On chalkboard or chart paper, make three columns. Over the first column, put an *A* and explain that this column is for situations in which you feel angry. Invite students to share some of the responses on their Anger Situations Forms. Select one situation for illustration. For example: "My little sister won't stay out of my stuff."
3. Over the second column, put a *B* and explain that this column is for the thoughts you have about the situation. Elicit several thoughts that might pertain to the situation. For example: "It's totally unfair that my sister keeps going in my room," "I'm gonna give her what she deserves," or "I can't stand it that she won't leave my stuff alone."
4. Over the third column, put a *C*. Explain that this column is for the feelings associated with the situation. Ask students how they think they would feel in this case. Responses might include "furious," "totally steamed," "like getting even," and so forth.
5. Ask students what they think would cause these feelings. Most will respond that the event (*A*) causes the feelings (*C*). Challenge this belief by inviting students to change the thoughts in the *B* column to more moderate ones. For example: "She's just a kid and doesn't know any better," "Big deal—it's not the end of the world that she gets in my stuff sometimes," or "Maybe I could get a padlock for my door." Ask students whether they would still feel as angry if they changed their thoughts about the situation.
6. Point out that situations (*A*'s) don't cause feelings (*C*'s) but that thoughts (*B*'s) cause feelings: No one forces us to be angry or tells us to be either a little angry or a whole lot angry. Suggest the idea that if you can change what you think about a situation, you can also change how you feel about it.

---

[2] The procedures described in Sessions 5 and 6 are based on the principles of rational-emotive therapy (RET). See the resources mentioned in the overview to this group for further information on this approach.

Closing Time

1. Invite students to pay attention to what they are thinking about situations and to consider how their thoughts may be causing them to feel and react more strongly than they might have to. Encourage them to continue to record anger-provoking events on their Anger Logs.
2. Ask whether there is anything anyone would like to say before the group ends and mention the topic of the next session (changing angry thinking). Remind students of the confidentiality rule and the time for the next meeting.

Changing Angry Thinking

Goals

1. To further illustrate how changing thoughts about a situation can change feelings as well
2. To give students practice in applying this technique to anger-provoking situations in their own lives

Materials

Anger Log (self-improvement exercise from Session 5)

Changing Angry Thinking Worksheet

Process

Review

1. Invite students to share how they feel about the idea of changing thoughts in order to change feelings. Review and discuss students' responses on their Anger Logs.

Working Time

1. Briefly describe the goals of the session.
2. Distribute copies of the Changing Angry Thinking Worksheet and explain that this form will help students practice modifying angry thoughts. Illustrate the use of the worksheet by going through one complete situation with students. For example:

   What happened

   My parents grounded me for the weekend because I left my bike out and it was stolen.

   What I thought

   I hate being grounded—now I can't go to the movies on Saturday. I can't stand losing my bike.

   What I felt

   Disappointed, furious, confused

   Changed thoughts

   I know better than to leave my bike out. It was my own fault I was grounded. I can deal with the disappointment.

   Changed feelings

   Sad, but resigned

3. Instruct students to pair up and work together to complete their worksheets. Urge them to choose real-life situations; circulate to provide help as needed.
4. After students have completed their worksheets, regroup to share situations, thoughts, and feelings. Discuss how the different thoughts might have changed students' feelings about the events.

Closing Time

1. Distribute new copies of the Changing Angry Thinking Worksheet and ask students whether they would be willing to record their thoughts and feelings about any difficult situations that may come up before the next session. Encourage them to continue to use their Anger Logs as needed.
2. Ask whether there is anything anyone would like to say before the group ends and mention the topic of the next session (taking personal responsibility for your own thoughts, feelings, and behaviors). Remind students of the confidentiality rule and the time for the next meeting.

Name________________________________ Date______________

Changing Angry Thinking Worksheet

Instructions: Write down the situation and your thoughts and feelings about the situation. Then write down what you could change your thoughts to and the new feeling you would have as a result.

Situation 1

What happened________________________________

____

What I thought________________________________

____

What I felt________________________________

____

Changed thoughts________________________________

____

Changed feelings________________________________

____

Situation 2

What happened________________________________

____

What I thought________________________________

____

What I felt________________________________

____

Changed thoughts________________________________

____

Changed feelings________________________________

____

Changing Angry Thinking Worksheet (cont'd)

Situation 3

What happened____

____

What I thought_______________________________________

____

What I felt____

____

Changed thoughts______________________________________

____

Changed feelings______________________________________

____

I'm in Charge of Me

Goals

1. To help students understand that each person is responsible for his or her own thoughts, feelings, and behaviors
2. To encourage students to state openly that they accept personal responsibility for their anger

Materials

Changing Angry Thinking Worksheet (self-improvement exercise from Session 6)

Anger Log (self-improvement exercise from Session 6)

A bowling ball

Process

Review

1. Invite students to share with the group their experiences in completing the Changing Angry Thinking Worksheet on their own. Were they successful in modifying angry feelings by changing their thoughts about a situation? If so, did having less intense feelings help them make a more appropriate and effective response? Encourage students to look for this possible connection in their completed Anger Logs.

Working Time

1. Briefly describe the goals of the session.
2. Explain that, when the group first began, some members might have believed that other people or situations caused anger but that we now know that we are responsible for our own thoughts, feelings, and behaviors. Accepting this idea means accepting *personal responsibility.*
3. Instruct students to sit in a circle on the floor. Explain that you will be using the bowling ball as a symbol of the heavy responsibility it is to be in charge of our own thoughts, feelings, and behaviors. Roll the bowling ball to one group member, then let students roll it back and forth among themselves a few times.
4. Taking the bowling ball back, explain that before you can roll the ball to someone else again, you must make a statement taking responsibility for yourself. Model this process by making one or two such statements. For example:
   - I am responsible for being irritable today because I didn't go to bed on time.
   - I am responsible for getting angry with the driver in front of me because I was late leaving for work.
   - I am responsible for feeling resentful because I didn't ask for what I want.
   - I am responsible for the unkind remark I made because I didn't stop and think first.
5. Roll the ball to someone who has self-disclosed in the past and who you believe will do so today. After this person has made a responsibility statement, he or she is to roll the ball to someone else in the group. The exercise continues until everyone has had a turn.
6. Ask the following discussion questions.
   - What was it like for you to make a statement taking personal responsibility?
   - How did you feel when someone else was taking a turn? While you were waiting for your turn?
   - How do you think making statements of personal responsibility might influence you in the future?
   - Why do you think people might not want to take responsibility for their own thoughts, feelings, and behaviors?

Closing Time

1. Encourage students to continue keeping their Anger Logs.
2. Ask whether there is anything anyone would like to say before the group ends and mention the topic of the final session (reviewing what has been learned in the group and saying goodbye). Remind students of the confidentiality rule and the time for the next meeting.

Saying Goodbye

Goals

1. To provide a review of what has happened in the past seven sessions
2. To help students understand and cope with the fact that the group is ending
3. To illustrate the importance of saying goodbye and give students a chance to achieve closure on the group and their relationships in it

Materials

Anger Log (self-improvement exercise from Session 7)

Construction paper in assorted colors (8 ½ × 11 inch sheets, cut in half)

Marking pens in assorted colors

Nutritious snack for everyone (raisins, fruit drink, etc.)

Process

Review

1. Ask students whether stating personal responsibility in Session 7 has had any effect on them and, if so, what that might be. Also invite students to share the experiences recorded on their Anger Logs since the last session. Praise them for their work thus far.
2. Next, go through the session topics and discuss what students feel are the most important lessons they learned in the group. The following questions may be helpful.
   - Where does anger come from? Is it ever possible for anger to be a good thing? What kinds of situations provoke your anger response? (Session 1)
   - What kind of anger clues could a person notice? *(situational, cognitive, physical)* What type of clues is it especially helpful for you to look out for? (Session 2)
   - What are some inappropriate ways to express anger? Some appropriate ways? Which way generally has better consequences? (Session 3)
   - What are *coping statements?* How can they help you control your anger? (Session 4)
   - What are the ABC's of anger? How can changing what you think about a situation change how you feel? (Sessions 5 and 6)
   - Who is in charge of your thoughts, feelings, and behaviors? Why is taking personal responsibility important? (Session 7)

Working Time

1. Point out that all relationships come to an end, whether by moving away or mutual decision, or for other reasons. Encourage students to talk about their own experiences with having relationships end.
2. Discuss the importance of goodbyes, stressing that saying goodbye can help people deal with sadness when a relationship ends and go on to new relationships. Explain that as a way of saying goodbye the group will be making special cards.
3. Show students how to make the cards by folding a piece of construction paper in half and, on the outside, writing "My Hope for You." Under that, write the name of a person in the group. On the inside, write a sentence or two of encouragement. For example: "Bill, my hope for you is that you will keep up the excellent gains in controlling your anger—you've done an outstanding job during the past weeks" or "Kim, my hope for you is that you have wonderful things happen because you can now take responsibility for your feelings."
4. Distribute the art materials. Take 15–20 minutes to construct similar cards for the other group members, and instruct students to do the same.

5. Reassemble the group, give out your cards to group members, and invite students to exchange cards among themselves.

Closing Time

1. Thank students for participating and remind them of the confidentiality rule. Tell students that, even though the group is ending, you will continue to be available to them (if indeed this is the case) and that you hope the friendships made in the group will continue.
2. Have a "group hug" if the atmosphere seems right, then share the snacks.

School Survival and Success

Youth spend approximately 10 thousand hours in the classroom from the time they start school until high school graduation. This experience is instrumental in shaping young persons' identity, self-esteem, social ability, career direction, values, and psychological well-being (Rutter, 1983; Santrock, 1987; Smith & Orlsky, 1975; Steinberg, 1985). Developmental psychologists are especially interested in studying issues associated with the academic transition from elementary to middle or junior high school because this transition coincides with a number of other major developmental changes: puberty, formal operational thought, increased independence from parents, and so forth.

As if these changes were not enough, young adolescents must also deal with a number of social changes that may affect their ability to cope academically. Some of these changes involve family instability, increased pressure for academic success, the ready availability of drugs, changing values and morals, and an increased sense of aloneness in the world. These factors may affect academic performance, motivation level, and frustration tolerance (Santrock, 1987). Frequently, youngsters are faced with more academic challenges than they have coping, communication, or social skills (Adams & Gullotta, 1989; Santrock, 1987).

Not surprisingly, research inquiries have indicated that the first year of middle school or junior high can be very stressful, both academically and socially. Classroom size, structure, and climate, as well as teacher personality traits, all appear to affect the young adolescent's education (Giaconia & Hedges, 1982; Hawkins & Berndt, 1985; Minuchin & Shapiro, 1983). The school counselor can soften the impact of this difficult transition period by providing support, encouragement, skills training, and an environment of trust in which the young adolescent can begin to overcome personal and academic difficulties.

Group Objectives

1. To give students the opportunity to be with peers at school who are working on their own personal and academic development
2. To help students learn how to manage their time more effectively
3. To illustrate the importance of setting learning goals and to define and develop long-, middle-, and short-term goals
4. To help students learn more effective classroom and study skills
5. To give students a chance to discuss stress surrounding tests and provide them with techniques to manage these feelings
6. To illustrate a method for effective decision making that students can use to make choices about situations relating to school
7. To help students understand how peer pressure can affect school performance and to demonstrate a method for saying no to destructive influences

Selection and Other Guidelines

The following target signs may indicate that a student is a candidate for this particular group experience.

1. Low self-esteem, as manifested by negative statements about self (e.g., "I'm fat, stupid, etc."), few or no friends, low motivation to succeed, and so forth
2. Poor adaptation in transferring from another school
3. Inability to cope with peer pressure surrounding academic performance (e.g., cheating, cutting class, etc.)
4. Poor ability to study
5. Extreme anxiousness when taking tests
6. General indecision in most situations

In addition to following the selection guidelines outlined in the Introduction, choose students with a range of abilities in academic skills. The major consideration is not to overload the group with youth who perform poorly in all areas; select students who are good in some areas but who need help in others.

The order of the sessions in this group is less crucial than it is in others. Sessions can stand alone, or they may be expanded upon as needed. Some of the members chosen for this group might require a whole series of sessions on certain topics. If necessary, more sessions can be added, or a whole group can be devised to revolve around a particular topic. Yet another alternative would be to develop a group guidance activity for a whole class. For example, activities to teach study and test-taking skills might be beneficial for a whole class.

Because these sessions are part of a group counseling experience, even though they contain procedures to reduce skill deficits, they are primarily driven by the need of members to deal with the emotional issues surrounding these deficits. It is therefore especially important in presenting the material to stress that group counseling is a forum in which feelings are first. Be sure to allow sufficient time in each session for processing group members' feelings about what is happening and what they are learning.

References and Recommended Reading

Adams, G. R., & Gullotta, T. (1989). *Adolescent life experiences.* Belmont, CA: Brooks/Cole.

Bartoletti, S., & Lisandrelli, E. (1988). *Study skills workout for grades 5–8.* Washington, MO: Paperbacks for Educators.

Berry, J. (1982). *Do your homework! (and schoolwork).* Washington, MO: Paperbacks for Educators.

Berry, J. (1987). *Every kid's guide to decision making and problem solving.* Washington, MO: Paperbacks for Educators.

Berry, J. (1987). *Every kid's guide to using time wisely.* Washington, MO: Paperbacks for Educators.

Canter, L. (1989). *Homework organizer for students.* Washington, MO: Paperbacks for Educators.

de la Sota, A. (1988). *Homework without tears for teachers grades 4–6.* Washington, MO: Paperbacks for Educators.

Fenker, R. (1981). *Stop studying, start learning.* Granbury, TX: Tangram Press.

Giaconia, R. M., & Hedges, L. V. (1982). Identifying features of effective open education. *Review of Educational Research, 52,* 579–602.

Hahn, J. (1985). *Have you done your homework? A parent's guide to helping teenagers succeed in school.* New York: Wiley.

Hawkins, J. A., & Berndt, T. J. (1985, April). *Adjustment following the transition to junior high school.* Paper presented at the biennial meeting of the Society for Research in Child Development, Toronto.

Minuchin, P. P., & Shapiro, E. K. (1983). The school as the content for social development. In P. H. Mussen (Ed.), *Handbook of child psychology* (Vol. 4, 4th ed.). New York: Wiley.

Purkey, W. W. (1970). *Self-concept and school achievement.* Englewood Cliffs, NJ: Prentice-Hall.

Rutter, M. (1983). School effects on pupil progress: Research findings and policy implications. *Child Development, 54,* 1–29.

Santrock, J. W. (1987). *Adolescence: An introduction* (3rd ed.). Dubuque, IA: Brown.

Schwartzrock, S. P. (1979). *Contemporary concerns of youth.* Circle Pines, MN: American Guidance Service.

Simon, S. B. (1974). *I am lovable and capable.* Chicago: Argus.

Smith, B. O., & Orlsky, D. E. (1975). *Socialization and schooling (Basics of reform).* Bloomington, IN: Phi Delta Kappa.

Solomon, A., & Grenoble, P. (1988). *Helping your child get top grades.* Washington, MO: Paperbacks for Educators.

Steinberg, L. (1985). *Adolescence.* New York: Knopf.

Getting Started

Goals

1. To help students become acquainted and begin to feel comfortable in the group setting
2. To choose appropriate ground rules for the group sessions
3. To identify why students want to be a part of the group and what they hope to learn
4. To help students become aware of how they spend their time and introduce the idea of time management

Materials

Chalkboard or chart paper
Sample Time Analysis Form
Time Analysis Form
A small "door prize" (box of raisins, ballpoint pen, coupon for a fast-food restaurant, etc.)

Process

Ice Breaker

1. Welcome students and briefly describe the goals of the group in general as well as this session in particular. Have group members pair up with the person on their right. Instruct pairs to share their names; their favorite food, TV show, song, and so forth (choose one or more areas); and what they hope to learn from coming to the group. Explain that students will be sharing this information with the whole group.
2. After about 5 minutes, reconvene the group. Ask members to introduce their partners and relate the information they learned.

Working Time

1. Introduce the idea of ground rules, pointing out that rules help everyone be respected and have time to talk. Suggest a few basic ground rules, such as the following.
   - What we say and do here is private and stays in the group (confidentiality rule).
   - Everyone has the right to "pass"—that is, not to participate in an activity or part of an activity.
   - No fighting or arguing.
   - Each person gets time to talk.
   - When someone is talking, everyone else will listen.
2. Ask students to think of other ground rules for the group. List all rules on the chalkboard or on chart paper.
3. Next ask, "How many of you would like to be better students?" (Most will giggle and raise their hands or otherwise agree.) Ask whether students would be willing to change some of the things they are doing now if it would mean they would become better students. These changes might involve getting rid of the following bad habits: studying infrequently, not preparing for tests, being unsure of homework assignments, forgetting to take books home to study, not having a special place and time to study at home, and so forth.
4. Explain that one important factor in doing better in school is learning to manage time efficiently. Ask students how much time and practice they think it takes to be a basketball player, musician, or actor. Point out that school success takes time also.
5. Distribute the Time Analysis Form. Stress that to make the best use of your day it is important to look at how you spend your time. (Perhaps you have large blocks of time that could be used to help you become a better student.) Ask students what kinds of things they do now during their time. The following discussion questions may help.

- When do you work? Play? Eat? Sleep?
- What happens to you when you get very busy and work too much?
- Have you known some adults who work too much? How do they behave?
- Do you think it is important to have fun time and loaf time? Why?
- What happens when a person does not organize time?
- How do you feel in the summer when there is "nothing to do?" What can you do about this feeling?

6. Explain that using the Time Analysis Form will help students get a better picture of what they do with their time. Then they can decide where to include the study time that suits them best.

Closing Time

1. Ask whether students would be willing to record what they do during their waking hours from now until the next time the group meets. Stress that it will take some self-discipline to do this: If they leave filling out the Time Analysis Form until night, they might forget what they did during certain periods of the day. Explain that students can use the codes on the form, if they like, or make up special codes to indicate the ways they spend their time. Using the Sample Time Analysis Form as an illustration will help students understand what is expected of them.
2. If time allows, challenge students to write down the names of everyone in the group before leaving. The person with the most names correct gets the "door prize." (If there is more than one winner, decide who gets the prize by drawing straws, picking a number between 1 and 10, etc.)
3. Ask whether there is anything anyone would like to say before the group ends and mention the topic of the next session (goal setting). Remind students of the confidentiality rule and the time for the next meeting.

Name *Cesar P.* Date *9/3/90*

Sample Time Analysis Form

Instructions: Use the following codes to write in your activities during the week. Make up your own codes for activities that are unique to you.

CL: Class time
F: Family activity
G: Goofing off by yourself
H: Doing a hobby
L: Taking a lesson
M: Mealtime
P: Playing with friends
S: Study time
SH: Shopping
SL: Sleeping
SP: Playing a sport
T: Talking on the telephone
TR: Travel time
TV: Watching TV
W: Working around the house
Other:

Time	Monday	Tuesday	Wednesday	Thursday	Friday	Saturday	Sunday
6 a.m.	SL	SL	SL	SL	SL	SL	SL
7 a.m.	M	M	M	M	M	SL	SL
8 a.m.	TR	TR	TR	TR	TR	SL	SL
9 a.m.	CL	CL	CL	CL	CL	SL	F
10 a.m.	CL	CL	CL	CL	CL	M	F
11 a.m.	CL	CL	CL	CL	CL	W	M
12 p.m.	M + P	M + P	M + P	M + P	M + P	W	TR
1 p.m.	L	CL	L	CL	L	SP	TR
2 p.m.	CL	CL	CL	CL	CL	SP	SP
3 p.m.	G	T	G	SP	SH	SP	SP
4 p.m.	T	SP	T	SP	SH	P	SP
5 p.m.	G	TV	G	M	M	M	M
6 p.m.	M	TV	M	TV	G	T	G
7 p.m.	S	W	H	G	TV	TV	T
8 p.m.	TV	G	S	G	TV	TV	TV
9 p.m.	TV	TV	TV	S	G	TV	TV
10 p.m.	SL	SL	SL	SL	SL	TV	SL
11 p.m.	SL	SL	SL	SL	SL	SL	SL

Name____ Date____________________

Time Analysis Form

Instructions: Use the following codes to write in your activities during the week. Make up your own codes for activities that are unique to you.

CL: Class time
F: Family activity
G: Goofing off by yourself
H: Doing a hobby
L: Taking a lesson
M: Mealtime
P: Playing with friends
S: Study time
SH: Shopping
SL: Sleeping
SP: Playing a sport
T: Talking on the telephone
TR: Travel time
TV: Watching TV
W: Working around the house
Other:

Time	Monday	Tuesday	Wednesday	Thursday	Friday	Saturday	Sunday
6 a.m.							
7 a.m.							
8 a.m.							
9 a.m.							
10 a.m.							
11 a.m.							
12 p.m.							
1 p.m.							
2 p.m.							
3 p.m.							
4 p.m.							
5 p.m.							
6 p.m.							
7 p.m.							
8 p.m.							
9 p.m.							
10 p.m.							
11 p.m.							

Goal Setting

Goals

1. To stress the importance of goals in achieving school success
2. To introduce the idea of long-, middle-, and short-term goals
3. To give students the opportunity to think through their own long-, middle-, and short-term goals

Materials

Time Analysis Form (self-improvement exercise from Session 1)
Red pens or pencils
Sample Goal-setting Worksheet
Goal-setting Worksheet
Chalkboard or chart paper

Process

Review

1. Invite students to share what they learned about themselves since the last session from filling out the Time Analysis Form. Ask the following questions.
   - Is there any time you could be studying when you aren't? When do you seem to be wasting the most time?
   - What would you be willing to change about the way you schedule your time to become a better student?
   - Do you study better in the morning, afternoon, or evening?
   - What days of the week is it easiest for you to schedule study time?
2. Distribute the red pens or pencils and instruct students to mark an *X* over those time periods they are willing to devote to improving themselves as students. This might mean getting tutoring, spending time in the library, getting help from a teacher or friend, and so forth.
3. Ask students for a verbal commitment to try to put their changes into effect. What do they think might happen if they do this?

Working Time

1. Briefly describe the goals of the session.
2. Ask students to imagine that their family is going on a trip to France for summer vacation. Discuss some of the decisions or steps that would be involved before the family could get to France.
   - How would they travel (train, plane, or car)?
   - What route should they take?
   - What factors should they consider in deciding when to go?
   - What should they take into account in deciding how much money to bring?
   - What kind of clothes would be best?
3. Point out that getting to France is the *goal,* and the decisions the family must make to reach this goal are the *plan.* Explain that in order to be a better student you also need a plan, or you might never reach your goals. Your plan is your "map" for reaching your goals.

4. Discuss the following questions.
   - What is a goal?
   - What do you think having goals would do for you?
   - Would you rather have goals or not have them?
   - What types of goals do you think there are?
5. Elicit that goals can be thought of in terms of the time it takes to reach them. In other words, they are *long term* (accomplished in years), *middle term* (accomplished in weeks or months), or *short term* (accomplished in weeks, days, or hours). Generate examples of each type. For example:

   Long-term goals
   - To go to college or get into the military
   - To become an astronaut
   - To graduate from high school
   - To get a good score on the SAT

   Middle-term goals
   - To pass algebra
   - To take driver's education
   - To pass band class then get into the marching band
   - To finish a science project on time

   Short-term goals
   - To come to group and not be too scared
   - To ask the gym teacher to let us play volleyball today
   - To pass a social studies test this afternoon
   - To make it through math without getting kicked out
6. Distribute copies of the Goal-setting Worksheet and invite the group to identify a possible long-term, middle-term, and short-term goal for becoming a better student. Write down these goals on the chalkboard or chart paper, then brainstorm the steps needed to reach them. (Use the Sample Goal-setting Worksheet as a model.)

Closing Time

1. Invite students to think of one long-, middle-, and short-term goal that would help them become better students. Ask them whether they would be willing to write these goals and the steps needed to reach them on their Goal-setting Worksheets. Let them know they will have the opportunity to share their ideas at the next session.
2. Discuss the following questions.
   - What did you learn in group today?
   - How could this help you be happier?
   - Are you willing to work on developing your goals?
   - After you have your goals outlined, what do you think it will take to get you started? What is keeping you from getting started?
   - What will it take for you to be successful in reaching goals?
   - What do you need to reach your goals that you don't have now?
3. Ask whether there is anything anyone would like to say before the group ends and mention the topic of the next session (getting the most out of class). Remind students of the confidentiality rule and the time for the next meeting.

Name *Sandy S.* Date *9/6/90*

Sample Goal-setting Worksheet

Instructions: Write down one long-term goal, one middle-term goal, and one short-term goal. Then write down the steps you think you will need to take to reach these goals.

Long-term Goal *To make the honor roll by the end of the year*

Steps

1. *Set aside an hour and a half each night to study.*
2. *Go to study and test-taking lab to improve skills.*
3. *Complete every assignment carefully and on time.*
4. *Get help soon in areas where I'm having problems.*
5. *Volunteer, select, and begin extra credit projects early.*

Middle-term Goal *To get at least a B on my science project*

Steps

1. *Read several sources about Saturn and its rings.*
2. *Make an outline of the written report.*
3. *Construct the planet and a stand to support it.*
4. *Have Mom proofread report; finish Saturn's rings.*
5. *Assemble project; take to school a day before it is due.*

Short-term Goal *To pass my math test next Friday*

Steps

1. *Get homework written down clearly.*
2. *Complete and turn in homework all week.*
3. *Ask Mr. Johnson for extra help on problems I don't understand.*
4. *Study during extra homework period.*
5. *Study extra for the test and do my best!*

Name____ Date__________________

Goal-setting Worksheet

Instructions: Write down one long-term goal, one middle-term goal, and one short-term goal. Then write down the steps you think you will need to take to reach these goals.

Long-term Goal ____

____

Steps

1. ____
2. ____
3. ____
4. ____
5. ____

Middle-term Goal ____

____

Steps

1. ____
2. ____
3. ____
4. ____
5. ____

Short-term Goal ____

____

Steps

1. ____
2. ____
3. ____
4. ____
5. ____

Getting the Most Out of Class

Goals

1. To present 10 skill areas for improving classroom performance
2. To give students an opportunity to rate themselves on these skills and identify areas where they need improvement
3. To provide practice in one of these skills (listening for test questions) and to encourage students to practice the others outside of the group

Materials

Goal-setting Worksheet (self-improvement exercise from Session 2)

Skills for Classroom Success Checklist

Process

Review

1. Invite students to share the goals and steps they listed on the Goal-setting Worksheet. Discuss whether the steps group members listed will help them reach their goals. Are students willing to get started on reaching these goals?

Working Time

1. Briefly describe the goals of the session.
2. Distribute copies of the Skills for Classroom Success Checklist. Ask students to take a few minutes to read each question and circle the number that best indicates how they feel they are at this time.
3. Go over each skill on the checklist. Explain that you will be giving students some ideas for how to improve in each area.

   Skill 1: I go to every class and get there on time.

   - If you are missing classes, ask yourself why and try to get some help with your situation (e.g., if your friends are pressuring you, have your counselor teach you skills to say no, or if you dislike the subject, talk it over with the teacher).

   Skill 2: I take a notebook to every class.

   - Write down important items and ideas.
   - Find out whether you are responsible for material in class lectures, what is in the book, or both.
   - Write down exactly what the homework is for each class and when it is due.

   Skill 3: I listen and concentrate in class.

   - Listen for main points and major ideas.
   - Listen for information about what will be on the test.
   - Sit in the front of the class if others distract you from listening.

   Skill 4: I ask questions when I need information.

   - It is your right to ask questions. Not doing so can result in your misunderstanding important ideas or being unsure of what you need to study for an exam.
   - Be sure you know what chapters a test will cover.
   - Find out what kind of questions will be on a test (multiple choice, short answer, recall information, word problems, etc.).

Skill 5: I take good notes in class.

- Don't think you can remember things the teacher said hours or days later—write them down in class.

Skill 6: I listen for possible test questions.

- Listen for cues and clues to test items.
- Write down examples the teacher gives.
- Write down lists of things (such as five types of invertebrates, six ways to give a speech, four great symphonies, etc.).
- If the teacher writes information on the chalkboard, it is probably important—write it down.
- Underline important words or definitions.
- If the teacher says something is important, this is a clue that the idea may be a possible test item.
- Listen for a change in the teacher's voice (verbal cues or clues). When something is very important, many teachers repeat it or say it louder, clearer, or slower so the class can write it down.

Skill 7: I participate actively in class.

- Teachers respond positively to students who seem interested. They also notice improved attitudes and behavior.
- Ask questions if you don't understand the material.
- Share your views on what is being said.
- If you are shy, make an agreement with yourself to say at least one thing in each class.

Skill 8: I understand what it will take to complete homework assignments.

- Write down assignments in a notebook.
- Ask questions if you are unsure of what you should do.
- Estimate the amount of time the homework will take to do and plan for it.

Skill 9: I have a "study buddy" in each class.

- Identify someone in every class who will agree to share information with you if you miss class.
- Write down this person's name, address, and phone number.

Skill 10: I practice good stress management before and after class.

- Practice relaxation exercises, thematic imagery, or positive coping statements (see Session 5 in this group and Sessions 4–7 in the group *Keeping Your Cool: Stress Management Skills*).
- Go to a quiet place to "get your head together" before an important class or test.
- Don't hang around kids who are saying negative things before a test.
- If you have a lot of things going on before an important class or test, set a time later on to worry about what is bothering you.
- If you are in an emotional crisis, go talk to your counselor.

4. Explain that you will next be conducting an experiment on listening for test questions (Skill 6). Select a passage from one of the textbooks students are currently using that clearly raises several major points or ideas. Read the passage aloud and ask group members to stop you when they hear something they think is an idea a teacher would ask on a test. Use your voice to emphasize topics that are "natural" test questions.

Closing Time

1. Discuss the following questions.

   - What did you learn about yourself in group today?
   - How can this help you to reach the goals you identified for yourself earlier?
   - Which of the 10 skills for classroom success do you think you will start working on right away?
   - Which of the skills are harder and might require more information before you can begin work on them?

2. Ask students whether they would be willing to practice some of these classroom skills and watch for any possible improvements.
3. Ask whether there is anything anyone would like to say before the group ends and mention the topic of the next session (study skills). Remind students of the confidentiality rule and the time for the next meeting.

Name____ Date____________________

Skills for Classroom Success Checklist

Instructions: Below are several skills that are important for doing well in class. Read each item, then circle the number of the response that is most like you at this time.

Scale 1 = I do very well

2 = I do well

3 = I do OK

4 = I need to improve some

5 = I need to improve a lot

1. I go to every class and get there on time.	1	2	3	4	5
2. I take a notebook to every class.	1	2	3	4	5
3. I listen and concentrate in class.	1	2	3	4	5
4. I ask questions when I need information.	1	2	3	4	5
5. I take good notes in class.	1	2	3	4	5
6. I listen for possible test questions.	1	2	3	4	5
7. I participate actively in class.	1	2	3	4	5
8. I understand what it will take to complete homework assignments.	1	2	3	4	5
9. I have a "study buddy" in each class.	1	2	3	4	5
10. I practice good stress management before and after class.	1	2	3	4	5

Study Skills

Goals

1. To present 10 skills for improving students' study performance
2. To give students an opportunity to rate themselves on these skills and identify areas where they need improvement
3. To encourage students to practice these skills outside the group

Materials

Skills for Classroom Success Checklist (self-improvement exercise from Session 3)

Skills for Study Success Checklist

Process

Review

1. Discuss students' experiences in trying out the classroom skills presented in Session 3, focusing on the following questions.
   - Did you notice any changes in your classroom behavior since the last session? What were these?
   - What happened as a result of your improvements?
   - Are these new skills something you are likely to continue? Why or why not?

Working Time

1. Briefly describe the goals of the session.
2. Distribute copies of the Skills for Study Success Checklist. Ask students to take a few minutes to read each question and circle the number that best indicates how they think they are at this time.
3. Go over each skill on the checklist. Explain that you will be giving students some ideas for how to improve in each area.

   Skill 1: I am aware of my own learning style.

   Learning style means how you go about the process of learning. Three things are important to look at when considering learning style.

   - How: Do you study best alone, with a friend, or in groups?
   - When: Do you study best in the morning, afternoon, or evening?
   - Where: Do you study best in study hall, alone in your room, at a table, lounging on the floor, at a friend's house, at the library, or at some other special place at home or school?

   Ask students to share how, when, and where they study best. Point out the range of individual differences.

   Skill 2: I set goals for my study time.

   Some examples of goals are as follows.

   - Review two chapters in English.
   - Organize notes from English class.
   - Decide on a topic for an English theme.
   - Make a brief outline of an English theme.

   Ask for volunteers to share examples of assignments, then generate appropriate study goals for them. Work through two or three examples.

Skill 3: I take good notes during class.

Ask what kind of information needs to be included in class notes. Possible responses include the following.

- Date of class
- Topic of discussion or lecture
- Major points (underlined, written in capital letters, or highlighted)
- Details or examples (written down in an orderly way—perhaps numbered)
- Information the teacher writes on the chalkboard

Skill 4: I carefully reread my class notes.

Students can make lists of words, definitions, or ideas they think will be on a test, or they can highlight these in their notes. They could also ask a study buddy what he or she thinks is important in the class notes.

Skill 5: I have effective reading skills.

Pretend to read silently from a passage, but move your lips while doing so. Ask group members what they notice about your reading (elicit that moving your lips while you read slows you down). Then model reading silently again, this time with a pencil placed horizontally in your mouth.

Skill 6: I know how to study a chapter effectively.

Ask students how they go about studying a specific chapter. Suggestions for improvement are as follows.

- Be sure to look at the headings and subheadings (usually in darker or larger print) before you begin reading.
- Check out all of the major topics the chapter covers.
- Read questions or summaries at the end of the chapter.
- Make notes on major topics and important words and concepts. (Writing things down gets the sense of touch involved in your learning and helps you learn quicker and remember longer.)
- Make a tape recording of important information and play it back.
- Read slower for new ideas and words; skim information you already know pretty well.

Skill 7: I study regularly.

Ask students what the phrase *cramming for an exam* means to them and why it is a good idea to study regularly instead. Possible responses might include the fact that leaving study to the last minute can make you feel overwhelmed, exhausted, or worried. In addition, you might not be able to concentrate well with so much to do, or you might forget information learned this way quicker than if you had taken the opportunity to repeat it over time.

Skill 8: I use my study time at school effectively.

Ask how students might use their time at school to better advantage. Suggestions for improvement are as follows.

- Identify a time at school that is wasted and could be used to study for an upcoming test.
- Check your schedule to eliminate large periods of unassigned time.
- Audiotape a lecture to play back later. (Be sure to ask permission before you tape a class!)

Skill 9: I spend enough time studying.

Discuss the following questions.

- Are the study times you set for yourself helping or hurting you in getting the job done?
- What could you do to use your time more effectively?
- How could you get more time to study?
- Could you study more some weeks when there aren't so many other activities to do and less some weeks when there are many interfering activities?

Skill 10: I plan a reward for myself after studying.

Ask how students could reward themselves after a study session or test. Examples might include eating ice cream, watching a favorite TV show, sharing positive feelings with someone, going somewhere special, and so forth.

Closing Time

1. Ask students whether they would be willing to practice some of these study skills. Which ones do they choose? What kind of changes might they expect if they practice these skills?
2. Ask whether there is anything anyone would like to say before the group ends and mention the topic of the next session (surviving tests). Remind students of the confidentiality rule and the time for the next meeting.

Name____ Date________________

Skills for Study Success Checklist

Instructions: Below are several skills that have to do with studying. Read each item, then circle the number of the response that is most like you at this time.

Scale 1 = I do very well

2 = I do well

3 = I do OK

4 = I need to improve some

5 = I need to improve a lot

1. I am aware of my own learning style.	1	2	3	4	5
2. I set goals for my study time.	1	2	3	4	5
3. I take good notes during class.	1	2	3	4	5
4. I carefully reread my class notes.	1	2	3	4	5
5. I have effective reading skills.	1	2	3	4	5
6. I know how to study a chapter effectively.	1	2	3	4	5
7. I study regularly.	1	2	3	4	5
8. I use my study time at school effectively.	1	2	3	4	5
9. I spend enough time studying.	1	2	3	4	5
10. I plan a reward for myself after studying.	1	2	3	4	5

Surviving Tests

Goals

1. To help students learn what stress is and become aware of why tests cause stress [1]
2. To encourage students to identify their own stress signs
3. To teach the use of deep breathing and thematic imagery as stress reduction techniques

Materials

Skills for Study Success Checklist (self-improvement exercise from Session 4)

Process

Review

1. Invite students to share experiences in practicing study skills. How did using these skills work out? What were the results, and how did students feel when they observed these results?

Working Time

1. Briefly describe the goals of the session.
2. Define *stress* as our body's reaction to both internal and external threats. *External threats* might include being harassed by a bully or being hurt in a car accident. The possibility that we might do poorly on an evaluation of some kind is perceived by most of us as an *internal threat* to our self-esteem. Generally, we want to get away from these kinds of stressors or fight them, so our body responds to get ready.
3. Ask students to explain how they know they are under stress. Some possible stress responses include increased pulse rate, perspiration, dilation of pupils, forgetting things you have studied, feeling "butterflies" in your stomach, and so forth.
4. Point out certain characteristics of tests that seem to be particularly stressful.
   - Having a time limit on the test
   - Being around other people who are anxious and saying negative things about the test
   - Not having enough time to prepare (as in the case of a "pop quiz")
   - Not having the materials you need to complete the test (e.g., pencil or pen, books, slide rule or calculator, etc.)
   - Saying negative things to yourself ("I can't do this"; "There's no way I'll pass")
   - Peer or family pressure to do well
   - Lack of self-confidence
   - Pressure to do well because the results are especially important (the SAT, a test for entrance into the military, etc.)
5. Explain that one good way to reduce the stress associated with a test is to be well prepared. If you have studied the material, you are more likely to be relaxed. However, a couple of specific techniques can also help: These are *deep breathing* and *thematic imagery*. Emphasize that these are aids, not to be used in place of study.
6. Explain that when we are under stress our breathing becomes shallow, our heart rate increases, and our muscles tighten. Illustrate how you can become more relaxed by slowing and deepening your breathing: Instruct students to put their hands over their diaphragms and notice the movement. Ask them to close their eyes and count how many breaths they take in a minute.

---

[1] Important background information on the nature of stress is included in the group *Keeping Your Cool: Stress Management Skills.*

Then model taking slower, deeper breaths and ask them to do the same. Time them again for a minute. (The number of breaths per minute should decrease.) Ask students whether they would be willing to try deep breathing the next time they find themselves feeling stress associated with a test.

7. Next, explain that thematic imagery can also help reduce stress associated with a test. This technique is based on the fact that the mind and body are connected. What we imagine or "picture" in our minds can help us change our body's response to stress. For example, if you imagine yourself in a quiet, peaceful place, your body is likely to respond with a slowed heart rate, relaxed muscles, and a feeling of calm. Ask students what kinds of scenes would be relaxing for them. Responses might include the following.
   - Playing on the beach
   - Walking in the woods
   - Sleeping in a hammock in the back yard
   - Riding a horse down by the river
   - Loafing out in the barn with your dogs
   - Watching the clouds slip over a mountain
   - Eating a favorite food
8. Ask group members to choose a quieting image, close their eyes, and imagine this scene, practicing deep breathing at the same time. Give them 3-4 minutes to become completely relaxed. Invite students to choose a posture conducive to relaxation (sitting on the floor, lying down in different places in the room, or just leaning back in their chairs).
9. Reassemble students in a circle and ask them to describe what it was like for them to practice deep breathing and thematic imagery.

Closing Time

1. Discuss the following questions.
   - What did you learn about stress and tests today?
   - What do you think about using deep breathing and thematic imagery to manage stress?
   - How do you think these techniques might help you?
2. Ask students whether they would be willing to practice deep breathing and thematic imagery before they fall asleep each night and before a stressful school-related activity or test, when the opportunity arises.
3. Ask whether there is anything anyone would like to say before the group ends and mention the topic of the next session (making better decisions). Remind students of the confidentiality rule and the time for the next meeting.

Making Better Decisions

Goals

1. To learn that decision making involves considering the risks, benefits, and consequences of choices
2. To give students a chance to practice a technique for making decisions

Materials

Sample Decision-making Worksheet
Decision-making Worksheet
Chalkboard or chart paper

Process

Review

1. Invite students to share their experiences in using deep breathing and thematic imagery in stressful school-related situations. Discuss the following questions.
   - How did it feel to practice these techniques?
   - What tests do you have coming up in the near future? How do you think using these techniques could help you prepare?
   - Do you think these approaches will work better for some tests than for others? Why?

Working Time

1. Briefly describe the goals of the session.
2. Ask students what kinds of decisions they need to make in school. These might concern subjects to take, activities to elect, schools to attend, report topics to choose, and so forth. Explain that *decision making* means choosing between alternatives and that it is a skill you can learn to do better with practice. (Even with practice, however, we may not always be able to make the best decisions for ourselves.)
3. Elicit questions students need to ask in order to make good decisions.
   - What are the choices involved?
   - Do I know everything I need to know about the situation? What information do I lack?
   - What are the possible risks and benefits that go along with each choice?
   - What are the final consequences of each choice?
   - How will I feel if I make one choice or another?
   - Which one of these choices is the best for me at this time?
4. Distribute copies of the Decision-making Worksheet and have students pair up and briefly discuss what school-related decisions each member of the pair will be facing in the near future. After about 5 minutes, reassemble as a group, then ask for volunteers to share their decisions. For example:
   - Should I take algebra (which is harder) or eighth-grade math (which is easier)?
   - Should I do an extra project in science to get a *B,* or should I be satisfied with doing less and getting a *C?*
   - Should I choose a teacher who is known to give a lot of work but who is interesting or a teacher who is easier but from whom I won't learn as much?
   - Should I ask a friend to study with me, or should I keep on the way I have been studying?

5. Choose one decision to illustrate the process outlined on the Decision-making Worksheet. As a group, brainstorm what information is needed and the risks, benefits, and consequences of the choices. Use the Sample Decision-making Worksheet as a guideline, encouraging everyone to participate and writing responses on the chalkboard or chart paper.
6. After the example decision has been worked through, discuss the following questions.
   - What was it like for you to share your decisions with a partner?
   - How do you usually go about making decisions? Is this new process a different experience for you?
   - How might this be a better way to make decisions?
   - How would you feel if you made a decision using this process and then later wished you had made another choice?

Closing Time

1. Ask whether students would be willing to fill out the rest of the Decision-making Worksheet to help them consider the risks, benefits, and consequences of the decisions they wrote down. Let them know they will have a chance to share this information at the next session.
2. Ask whether there is anything anyone would like to say before the group ends and mention the topic of the next session (coping with peer pressure). Remind students of the confidentiality rule and the time for the next meeting.

Name *Becky R.* Date *9/27/90*

Sample Decision-making Worksheet

Instructions: Write down your decision statement, the two choices in your decision, and the possible risks and benefits for each choice. Then write down your final decision and your reasons behind it.

Decision Statement *Should I do an extra science project to bring up my grade to a B, or should I be satisfied with doing less and getting a C?*

Choice #1 *Do the extra science project*

Risks	Benefits
Doing the project is not a guarantee of a better grade.	*A better grade would help balance my lower grades.*
It will take several weekends of work to finish.	*I like science and have fun doing the projects.*
I might have to do the project all myself, and I don't think I can complete it alone.	*My dad usually helps me—I'd get to spend more time with him.*

Choice #2 *Don't do the extra science project*

Risks	Benefits
Not getting at least a B could hurt my chances of getting into college.	*I'll have more free time.*
	I can concentrate on other subjects.
My teacher and parents might be mad at me if I don't do it.	*I won't have to work so hard.*
	I won't have to work with a teacher I dislike.

Consequences

Choice #1 *I'll have to give up some free time and some fun activities, but I'll probably get a B for the course. If I do get my grade up, I'll be proud of myself.*

Choice #2 *I'll have lots of time to devote to fun things and other subjects, but I'll probably get a C for the course and feel guilty for not doing the work.*

My Decision *I'll go ahead and do the extra project because it is more important for the long run for me to have a chance to get my science grade up than it is to have the extra free time.*

Name____ Date____________________

Decision-making Worksheet

Instructions: Write down your decision statement, the two choices in your decision, and the possible risks and benefits for each choice. Then write down your final decision and your reasons behind it.

Decision Statement ____

____

Choice #1 ____

Risks	Benefits
____________________	____________________
____________________	____________________
____________________	____________________
____________________	____________________

Choice #2 ____

Risks	Benefits
____________________	____________________
____________________	____________________
____________________	____________________
____________________	____________________

Consequences

Choice #1 ____

____

Choice #2 ____

____

My Decision ____

____

____

Coping with Peer Pressure

Goals

1. To give students a chance to discuss different kinds of peer pressure
2. To illustrate how peer pressure relates to school performance
3. To allow students to practice saying no and/or leaving situations in which they are being pressured

Materials

Decision-making Worksheet (self-improvement exercise from Session 6)

Index cards

Process

Review

1. Discuss students' experiences in using the Decision-making Worksheet, using the following questions.
   - How did your decision-making plan work out?
   - What do you think you could have done differently?
   - How do you think you could use this decision-making process in the future?

Working Time

1. Briefly describe the goals of the session.
2. Explain that learning to say no is an important skill to use in avoiding peer pressure. Invite students to generate some examples of situations in which they feel pressured. These might involve the use of drugs or alcohol, rule breaking or illegal activities, demands for certain types of behavior, and so forth.
3. Brainstorm ways to say no. For example:
   - Look directly at the person and say, "No" or "No, thanks."
   - Laugh and say, "You've got to be kidding."
   - Say, "No way," then turn and walk away without looking back.
   - Say, "That's not for me."
   - Say, "I'm sorry, I won't do that."
   - If a person persists, repeat any of the above exactly (broken-record technique).
   - If someone heckles you, look straight ahead and walk away. (Look forward, not up or down. This gives the message that you mean what you say, won't change your mind, and don't feel bad about saying no.)
4. Point out that a good deal of peer pressure can surround school performance, and that it is important for students to be able to stand up for themselves and resist this pressure. Ask students to pair up, then give each pair an index card on which you have written one of the following role-play situations.
   - Your friend asks you to give her your homework to copy.
   - Your older brother wants you to use his science project as your own so you will have time to do his chores for him.
   - Some kids at school ask you to go to the shopping mall with them, but you have extra homework to do tonight.
   - The most popular girl at school asks you if you will steal a copy of the test on the teacher's desk and give it to her.

- A kid at band practice says he will break your good dress hat if you don't give him 5 dollars.
- Your best friend asks you to study with her, but you know that when you study together time gets wasted and no studying gets done.
- Your three best friends ask you to skip class and goof off.

5. Instruct pairs to choose who will play which role and together devise a way to say no to the request. After a few minutes, reassemble the group and have pairs perform their role plays. Discuss whether or not students feel the responses will be effective, allowing everyone a chance to participate. Emphasize the idea that it is often difficult to say no under pressure.

Closing Time

1. Discuss the following questions.
   - What did you learn about saying no?
   - What did you learn about peer pressure?
   - Do you think saying no in the ways illustrated would work for you?
2. Ask whether students would be willing to try saying no sometime between now and the next session. What kind of situations do they anticipate?
3. Ask whether there is anything anyone would like to say before the group ends and mention the topic of the final session (reviewing what has been learned in the group and saying goodbye). Remind students of the confidentiality rule and the time for the next meeting.

Saying Goodbye

Goals

1. To provide a review of what has happened in the past seven sessions
2. To help students understand and cope with the fact that the group is ending
3. To illustrate the importance of saying goodbye and give students a chance to achieve closure on the group and their relationships in it

Materials

Nutritious snack for everyone (raisins, fruit drink, etc.)

Process

Review

1. Invite students to share their experiences saying no in a peer pressure situation. What were the results of their standing up for themselves? How did it feel to express themselves in this way?
2. Next, go through the session topics and discuss what students feel are the most important lessons they learned in the group. The following questions may be helpful.
   - What did you learn about managing your time better? Have you made any changes in the way you do things as a result of thinking about how you spend your time? (Session 1)
   - Has the Goal-setting Worksheet been helpful to you? Has anyone set any goals or made any decisions about working toward goals? (Session 2)
   - What classroom and study skills did you learn about? Did making changes in these areas have any impact on your school performance? On how you see yourself as a student? (Sessions 3 and 4)
   - What is stress and why do we sometimes feel stress when we have to take tests? Has using deep breathing and/or thematic imagery helped you reduce your stress? (Session 5)
   - What should you think about when you make decisions relating to school? *(risks, benefits, consequences)* (Session 6)
   - Do you think peer pressure affects how you see yourself as a student? What can you do about this? (Session 7)

Working Time

1. Point out that all relationships come to an end, whether by moving away or mutual decision, or for other reasons. Encourage students to talk about their own experiences with having relationships end.
2. Discuss the importance of goodbyes, stressing that saying goodbye can help people deal with sadness when a relationship ends and go on to new relationships.
3. Model saying goodbye by sharing a positive statement about each group member. For example: "Randy, I believe you will make great progress in your classes now that you know more about how to organize your time" or "Dawn, keep up the good work setting goals for yourself!"
4. Invite each student to make similar positive statements about fellow group members.

Closing Time

1. Thank students for participating and remind them of the confidentiality rule. Tell students that, even though the group is ending, you will continue to be available to them (if indeed this is the case) and that you hope the relationships made in the group will continue.
2. Have a "group hug" if the atmosphere seems right, then share the snacks.

Coping with Grief and Loss

Although the topic of death has long been taboo in our society, we must all face this end to the life cycle eventually. * The death of someone we care for can leave confusing and unresolved feelings in those left behind. Learning to resolve these issues has been recommended by many mental health professionals (Beebe, 1971; Feifel, 1982; Irish, 1971; Kalish, 1985; Kubler-Ross, 1975; Stillion, 1983; Zalaznik, 1986).

Certain problems exist in attempting to meet this need in the school setting, however. As suggested by McClure (1974), the topic of death evokes powerful emotions that the individuals involved in such a learning situation might not be able to handle. Second, this topic is heavily value-laden and might easily become controversial. Another problem could be the lack of preparation of those carrying out the grief counseling activities. Finally, due to a lack of empirically validated research on such instruction, administrative and parental support might be lacking.

Despite such difficulties, the well-trained school counselor can be a central figure in the provision of counseling services to youngsters who have experienced this kind of loss. In fact, the school counselor is frequently the person to whom others in the school setting go for help in dealing with the academic and emotional problems that arise when death affects someone in the learning community. Pressure to "do something" for the grieving person or persons and a genuine desire to help are reasons the school counselor would want to become educated and involved in providing such services.

Group Objectives

1. To provide students with a forum for discussing their feelings about the death or serious illness of someone they care for
2. To help students understand what death is, different causes of death, and the idea of death as part of the natural cycle
3. To illustrate the importance in all cultures of a special public ritual to memorialize the person who has died and to provide an opportunity for students to discuss their ideas and feelings about funerals
4. To give students the chance to create and share their own personal memorials
5. To describe some of the basic emotions associated with loss and to provide time for students to discuss these feelings
6. To help students understand death by suicide, especially the reasons involved, warning signs, and what to do if they or someone they know is thinking of suicide
7. To help students become aware that they have a choice between self-destructive behaviors like suicide and more positive methods of coping with loss

Selection and Other Guidelines

Death education—often provided in a class on such subjects as family living, health, and psychology is a guidance activity offered regardless of whether or not a loss has been experienced. In contrast, the goal of this group experience is primarily remedial, and participants are selected because they are in the process of dealing with issues surrounding a specific loss or anticipated loss.

In addition to following the selection guidelines outlined in the Introduction, you will therefore be choosing students who have experienced the death or serious illness of a family member or friend. You may also wish to include students who have a relationship with a very elderly family member or friend, even though that person is not presently ill. Some target signs that indicate a student may be having difficulty dealing with this kind of loss or imminent loss are as follows.

1. The inability to stop talking about the death or illness
2. Denial that the loss has or will take place
3. Sudden withdrawal or refusal to socialize
4. A joking facade (e.g., talking about ghosts, skeletons, etc.)
5. A change in the level of risk-taking behaviors
6. Classical signs of depression (e.g., trouble sleeping or eating, difficulty concentrating, apathy, etc.)

* Special credit should go to Dr. Judith M. Stillion for her thoughtful commentary on early versions of these group procedures. Dr. Stillion, a past president of the Association for Death Education and Counseling, is a professor of psychology and Associate Vice Chancellor for Academic Affairs at Western Carolina University.

It is very important to avoid selecting students who are still in a state of shock from the death of a significant person, who are experiencing a family crisis of some kind, or who have attempted suicide or are actively talking about doing so. (Item 8 on the pretest/posttest can help you screen out students who are potentially suicidal.)

In addition, the youth selected for this group can be considered to be high risk for further emotional problems or acting-out behavior. Be sure that you, the students, and the students' parents are aware of this possibility. Make it very clear that you will provide individual counseling if needed or that you will refer youngsters to a professional competent in dealing with grief issues. You might want to provide students and their parents with a list of counselors in your area who provide this type of service before the group even begins.

Yet another important issue concerns counselor preparation. Before undertaking this kind of group, a certain level of mastery must be achieved. Specifically, such mastery involves the following.

1. A study of the developmental process of how children and adolescents experience death on cognitive, affective, and behavioral levels
2. An awareness of the social and psychological issues that arise when dealing with the topic of death
3. An examination of how you have dealt personally with the issues of death, loss, and grief and a willingness to be open about these issues
4. Willingness to "be there" for group members who may experience deep emotions during the counseling process
5. A thorough understanding of group process, including techniques to facilitate trust, cohesion, universality, and hope
6. A clear line of communication with the parents and teachers of the students involved
7. The ability to handle moral or religious questions associated with death and dying
8. Specialized training in the area of death and loss, such as that obtained through advanced coursework or participation in workshops and seminars [1]

Finally, a discussion of death is not complete without including the topic of suicide. Social changes have increasingly led youngsters to take their own lives rather than face discouragement, hopelessness, decimated self-esteem, and loss. Session 6 in this group counseling series is devoted to understanding some of the important issues associated with suicide, both from the perspective of the person contemplating this course and from the viewpoint of the people left behind after a suicide. Again, mastery of the literature on this topic is an important prerequisite for conducting this session.

References and Recommended Reading

Beebe, L. (1971). Sudden death. In B. R. Green & D. P. Irish (Eds.), *Death education: Preparation for living.* Rochester, VT: Schenkman.

Bennett, R. (1974, April). *Death and the curriculum.* Paper presented at the annual meeting of the American Educational Research Association, Chicago.

Berman, A. L. (1988). Playing the suicide game. *Readings: A Journal of Reviews and Commentary in Mental Health, 3,* 20–23.

Buscaglia, L. (1982). *The fall of Freddie the leaf.* Thorofare, NJ: Slack.

Engel, G. L. (1980). A group dynamics approach to teaching and learning about grief. *Omega: Journal of Death and Dying, 11,* 45–49.

Feifel, H. (1982). Death in contemporary America. *Death Education, 6,* 105–174.

Gibson, A. B. (1982). *Death education: A concern for the living.* Bloomington, IN: Phi Delta Kappa.

Grollman, E. A. (1976). *Talking about death: A dialogue between parent and child.* Boston: Beacon.

Irish, D. P. (1971). Death education: Preparation for living. In B. R. Green & D. P. Irish (Eds.), *Death education: Preparation for living.* Rochester, VT: Schenkman.

Joan, P. (1986). *Preventing teenage suicide.* New York: Human Sciences.

[1] The Association for Death Education and Counseling provides such certification programs. For details, contact the association at 638 Prospect Avenue, Hartford, CT 06105.

Kalish, R. A. (1985). *Death, grief, and caring relationships* (2nd ed.). Belmont, CA: Brooks/Cole.

Kubler-Ross, E. (1969). *On death and dying.* London: Macmillan.

Kubler-Ross, E. (1975). *Death: The final stage of growth.* Englewood Cliffs, NJ: Prentice-Hall.

Kubler-Ross, E. (1983). *On children and death.* New York: Collier/Macmillan.

Kushner, H. S. (1983). *When bad things happen to good people.* New York: Avon.

McClure, J. W. (1974). Death education. *Phi Delta Kappan, 7,* 483–485.

Orbach, I. (1988). *Children who don't want to live: Understanding and treating the suicidal child.* San Francisco: Jossey-Bass.

Pfeffer, D. R. (1986). *The suicidal child.* New York: Guilford.

Rando, T. A. (1984). *Grief, dying, and death: Clinical interventions for caregivers.* Champaign, IL: Research Press.

Raphael, B. (1983). *The anatomy of bereavement.* New York: Basic.

Rofes, E. (1985). *The kid's book about death and dying.* Boston: Little, Brown.

Rosenthal, N. R. (1981). Attitudes toward death education and counseling. *Counselor Education and Supervision, 20,* 203–210.

Sarafino, E. P. (1986). *The fears of childhood.* New York: Human Sciences.

Stillion, J. M. (1983). Where thanatos meets eros: Parallels between death education and group therapy. *Death Education, 7,* 53–67.

Stillion, J. M., McDowell, E. E., & May, J. H. (1989). *Suicide across the lifespan: Premature exits.* New York: Hemisphere.

Stillion, J. M., & Wass, H. (1984). Children and death. In E. S. Schneidman (Ed.), *Death: Current perspectives.* Palo Alto, CA: Mayfield.

Wass, H. (1985). *Death education: An annotated resource guide.* New York: Hemisphere.

Zalaznik, P. W. (1986). Dimensions of loss and death education. A resource and curriculum guide. Minneapolis: EDU-PAC.

Getting Started

Goals

1. To help students become acquainted and feel comfortable in the group setting
2. To choose appropriate ground rules for the group sessions
3. To identify why students want to be a part of the group and what they hope to learn
4. To help students begin to understand and express the feelings associated with their loss

Materials

Feelings Chart (from the group *Dealing with a Divorce in the Family,* p. 24)
Chalkboard or chart paper
Drawing paper
Marking pens in assorted colors

Process

Ice Breaker

1. Welcome students and briefly describe the goals of the group in general as well as this session in particular.
2. Ask group members to share their names and something about the person in their lives who has died or who is very ill or elderly. Let them take as long as they need to express this information. The types of responses students might make include the following.
   - "My grandpa died this past summer. I used to go to his house every weekend to visit him and Grandma and help feed his cows. I miss him very much."
   - "My friend Peter died of leukemia last year. He was 13 years old."
   - "My aunt Hilda lives with us. She has cancer, and my mom and dad said she won't live very much longer."
3. Invite students to discuss what they hope to learn from the group.

Working Time

1. Introduce the idea of ground rules, pointing out that rules help everyone be respected and have time to talk. Suggest a few basic ground rules, such as the following.
   - What we say and do here is private and stays in the group (confidentiality rule).
   - Everyone has the right to "pass"—that is, not to participate in an activity or part of an activity.
   - No fighting or arguing.
   - Each person gets time to talk.
   - When someone is talking, everyone else will listen.
2. Ask students to think of other ground rules for the group. List all rules on the chalkboard or on chart paper.
3. Next, distribute copies of the Feelings Chart. Talk a few minutes about how feelings come in different intensities: high, moderate, or low.
4. Distribute the drawing paper and marking pens. Instruct students to fold the paper in half vertically, then horizontally. (The paper will now contain four rectangles.) Ask group members to write a feeling associated with the death or illness situation in each of the four rectangles. Encourage them to consult the Feelings Chart as needed. Finally, as shown on the next page, ask students to draw in each rectangle a circle face that expresses their feelings.

Feeling Faces

5. Invite students to share their drawings and to talk about the feelings they have experienced. Expect a range of self-disclosure: Some students won't know how they feel, and some will be reluctant to say because they may not want to admit their feelings or they may be afraid of what others will think.
6. Encourage discussion by asking the following questions.
   - What kinds of feelings do students in this group have about the death or illness of their friend or family member?
   - Is it OK to have these feelings?
   - What kinds of feelings do you have? Are they the same or different from others' feelings?
   - Why might it help if you talk about your feelings with other people?
   - What is the scariest thing about coming to group? The nicest thing?

Closing Time

1. Make a positive statement to each group member about his or her participation. For example: "Kyle, I'm glad you shared your feelings about your grandpa—welcome to the group" or "Beth Ann, I hope we will be able to work together to understand what your friend's death means to you."
2. Ask whether there is anything anyone would like to say before the group ends and mention the topic of the next session (what death is and how it happens). Tell students that you will be available if they need you between sessions and remind them of the confidentiality rule and the time for the next meeting.

What Is Death and How Does It Happen?

Goals

1. To help students understand the legal definition of death and encourage them to define death in their own terms
2. To help students realize that death is an inevitable part of the natural cycle
3. To promote an understanding of the different causes of death (illness, accident, deliberate action) and how these different circumstances can affect how people feel about a death

Materials

Chalkboard or chart paper

Process

Review

1. Ask students whether they can remember any of the feelings discussed during the last session. Invite them to share any additional feelings or thoughts they might be having.

Working Time

1. Briefly describe the goals of the session.
2. Ask students to define *death* in their own way. Some possible responses are as follows.

   - When your heart stops beating.
   - When you stop breathing.
   - When your brain stops.
   - When the doctor says you are dead.
   - When God takes your soul.
   - I don't know.
   - When you get shot.

   Take care to acknowledge each idea with a positive affirmation like "OK," "I see," "good idea," and so forth. The technique of minimal acknowledgment is especially helpful in dealing with responses having religious or value-laden content.

3. After giving students ample time to generate their own definitions, explain that the legal definition of death means that a person's brain has stopped giving off certain electrical signals or "brain waves." Even if a person can't breathe without the help of a machine, that person is still considered alive until the brain has died. Allow students to react to this idea. (Perhaps a student in the group has known someone who has been on a respirator.)
4. Ask whether people are the only thing in the world that dies. Point out that dying is part of nature: In the spring, nature renews itself by sending new plants into the sunshine. In summer, plants grow, getting stronger and developing seeds so they can make more of their species. In the autumn, the seeds fall and the plant loses its strength. Finally, winter comes and the plant dies. Elicit the correspondence between the seasons and various stages of the lifespan: infancy, youth, middle age, and old age. Discuss how everything in nature (plants, insects, animals, people) follows this cyclic pattern.
5. Ask students to explain how people die. Elicit that death can happen in old age, but it can also happen as a result of *illness* (e.g., cancer, heart attack), *accident* (e.g., automobile crash, drowning), or *deliberate action* (e.g., suicide, homicide, war). Write these three categories on the chalkboard or chart paper and help students generate a list of possible ways death could occur in each.

6. Discuss the following questions.
   - Do you think you would feel different if you knew someone died in one of these ways rather than in another?
   - What is it like when someone dies unexpectedly?
   - How is an unexpected death different from when someone dies in old age?
   - Do you know anyone who has died after a long illness? What was being ill like for the person? For the person's friends and family?

Closing Time

1. Ask students to summarize what they think was most important about the group discussion today.
2. Ask whether there is anything anyone would like to say before the group ends and mention the topic of the next session (feelings that come with loss). Tell students you will be available if they need you between sessions and remind them of the confidentiality rule and the time for the next meeting.

Feelings That Come with Loss

Goals

1. To acquaint students with some of the major emotions associated with loss
2. To give students the opportunity to see how these emotions can be experienced by the dying person as well as by friends and family
3. To help students recognize and understand these emotions in themselves

Materials

Chalkboard or chart paper

Process

Review

1. Ask students whether they have had any additional thoughts about death being a natural part of life or ways in which death happens. Discuss.

Working Time

1. Briefly describe the goals of the session.
2. Explain that an author named Elizabeth Kubler-Ross wrote a book entitled *On Death and Dying.* Explain that Kubler-Ross studied many dying people and their families and developed an interesting theory about what feelings dying people and their loved ones have. [2]
3. Discuss the following emotions, noting each on chalkboard or chart paper as it is brought up.

Denial

Denial is experienced when someone does not want to believe that something awful has happened or is about to happen. People who are going to die often have feelings of denial. For example, suppose a person receives information from his doctor that his lab tests show he has an incurable and terminal disease. The person might say, "The lab tests must be wrong. They must be someone else's—they can't be mine." When a person dies suddenly, those left behind are also often left with feelings of disbelief and denial.

Point out that sometimes denial can be healthy, as is the case when saying, "I can lick this thing" helps a person fight a serious illness and live longer. Denial could be unhealthy if it keeps people from resolving important issues before their death (like making a will) or if it keeps friends or family from being able to talk about their feelings or say goodbye.

- Do you know anyone who might have denied he or she had a serious illness or that there was a serious illness in the family?
- Do you think denial is good or bad?
- Do we ever try to deny that other bad things can happen (e.g., having to move to a new town, getting a bad grade, having a girlfriend or boyfriend break up with you)?

Isolation

Isolation means feeling all alone and misunderstood or lacking people to support and comfort you. A person who has to deal with a serious illness and thoughts of his or her own death might

[2] The major emotions presented here have been adapted from *On Death and Dying,* by Elizabeth Kubler-Ross, 1969, London: Macmillan. Kubler-Ross originally conceptualized these emotions as stages of dying. Because the sequential nature of these "stages" has not been supported by research or caregivers, it is important to treat these areas as emotions that may occur and reoccur at any time.

feel very alone at times. The friends and family of such a person might also feel that no one else can comfort them or understands what they are going through.

- Has anyone you have known who has been very ill or who has died ever felt isolated? How did the person show this feeling?
- Have you ever tried to comfort someone who is very ill or dying or who has lost someone close? What did you do or say? Were you able to help?
- Have you ever felt isolated? What did you do to try to feel better?

Anger

It is normal to feel angry when you are losing something. A person who is seriously ill has to think of losing life, whereas those left behind when a person dies lose someone they care for. Anger can be expressed in many ways. For example, someone who is ill could lash out at family, friends, or medical staff. Or the person could feel resentful, asking, "Why me instead of someone else?"

- Has anyone you have known who has been very ill or who has died ever felt angry? How did the person show this feeling?
- Have you ever felt angry that someone you cared for might die or has died?
- Can you help someone who is angry in this way? What could you do for yourself if you are angry?

Bargaining

Suppose your mother said you had to clean out the basement on Saturday. The basement is a disaster area, so you bargain and negotiate with your mom to let you clean it out the first rainy Saturday that comes along. You promise you won't ask for another postponement when that Saturday comes, and you remind your mom how good you have been in order to persuade her to let you make this bargain.

People who are dying also sometimes try to "strike deals" to gain more time. They may say to themselves or to God, "Just give me one more pain-free day" or "I only want to hang on long enough to see my daughter's wedding." Most such bargains are made privately, and other people seldom know about them. Family and friends can also bargain. For example, a mother might try to bargain for another month or so until her child's birthday.

- Have you ever tried to make a bargain like this? What happened?
- Why do you suppose a dying person might want to make a bargain?
- What do you think the person is bargaining for?
- Do you think such bargains are ever kept?

Depression

When a person experiences a loss, there may be a deep and lasting feeling of sadness. A person who is ill may have many losses: With a deterioration in health may come loss of ability to do physical things or to control bodily functions. There may also be pain, as well as a loss of material goods, the comfort of being in one's own home, and self-esteem.

These losses can add up to depression, both for the person experiencing the illness and for the people around him or her.

- Has anyone you have known who has been very ill or who has anticipated death ever felt depressed? How did the person show this feeling?
- Have you ever felt depressed when you thought about someone who might die or who has died?
- Can you help someone who is depressed in this situation? What could you do to help yourself if you feel depressed?

Acceptance

Acceptance means that you have come to terms with the fact that death happens to everyone. It is possible for dying people and those around them to feel acceptance in some situations. In other situations, acceptance may not be possible.

- Has anyone you have known who has been very ill or who has anticipated death accepted this situation? How did the person show this feeling?
- Have you ever felt acceptance when you thought about someone who might die or who has died?
- What do you think would have to happen in order for a person to be able to feel acceptance? What might happen if a person is unable to accept the loss?

4. Throughout the discussion, emphasize the idea that these emotions may occur and reoccur throughout the process of dying. For example, one day your grandparent may be ready to talk about death; the next, he or she may deny its imminence. People react to these kinds of challenges quite differently, and responses cannot be expected to follow an orderly, prescribed sequence. In addition, stress that if friends and family know a person is going to die it is possible for them to experience these emotions long before the death actually takes place (anticipatory grief).

Closing Time

1. Discuss how knowing about these emotions might help a person deal with loss. Stress that these feelings are normal and that understanding them might help the person know what to expect. Invite students to talk about what they have learned about themselves today.
2. Ask whether there is anything anyone would like to say before the group ends and mention the topic of the next session (the importance of the funeral). Tell students you will be available to them between sessions and remind them of the confidentiality rule and the time for the next meeting.

The Importance of the Funeral

Goals

1. To give students a chance to discuss their experiences in attending funerals
2. To help students understand the importance of the funeral ritual in dealing with death
3. To illustrate that all cultures share the need to memorialize those who have died

Materials

Flyers or pamphlets from a local funeral home describing different funeral arrangements
Photographs and descriptions of burial rites in various cultures [3]

Process

Review

1. Remind students that in the last session they learned about some of the emotions that can accompany loss. Invite students to share any additional observations on these emotions. Did learning about these feelings help them in any way? Were they able to use this information?

Working Time

1. Briefly describe the goals of the session.
2. Discuss what happens after a person is declared legally dead: Most of the time, the body is taken to a funeral home. The family members talk with the funeral director to make arrangements for burial or cremation. A casket or urn is selected, and if a religious service is to be held, plans are made for it.
3. Distribute flyers or pamphlets from a local funeral home. Invite students to discuss the options described in them and to share their experiences in attending funerals. The following discussion questions may help.
   - What funerals have you attended? What was your relationship to the person(s) who died?
   - Do you remember what took place at the funeral? Was there a time for visiting the body at the funeral home or did everything take place at the cemetery?
   - If the family planned on having the body buried, was there an open or closed casket? Do you see any advantages in having the casket open? *(It might help some people understand that the person is really dead and to say goodbye.)* Which would you prefer if you had a choice?
   - Do you know of anyone who has been cremated? How do you feel about this option?
   - Did attending the funeral help you or other family members and friends in any way? How do you think feelings might have been different if there were no funeral?

   Students may be very curious about the details surrounding death and burial (how the corpse looks, embalming, etc.). This curiosity is natural; take care to answer these types of questions as fully as you can.
4. After allowing students time to discuss their personal experiences and feelings, describe the funeral customs of several other cultures, showing photographs whenever possible. Invite students to express their feelings about these rituals and to discuss what points are similar to and different from funeral rituals in our own culture. Elicit the idea that people in all cultures need to *memorialize* (find a special way to remember) those who have died.

---

[3] One good resource for this session is the filmstrip *Funeral Customs around the World*, included in the multi-media kit *Perspectives on Death*, by D. W. Berg and G. G. Daugherty, 1972, DeKalb, IL: Educational Perspectives Associates.

Closing Time

1. Thank students for sharing their personal experiences in attending funerals.
2. Ask whether there is anything anyone would like to say before the group ends and mention the topic of the next session (creating a personal memorial). Tell students you will be available to them between sessions and remind them of the confidentiality rule and the time for the next meeting.

A Personal Memorial

Goals

1. To provide students with an opportunity to create a lasting document expressing their feelings about the person who is ill or who has died
2. To allow students to share these feelings with other group members and to illustrate that others share similar feelings

Materials

Drawing paper
Marking pens in assorted colors
Construction paper in assorted colors
Glue
Scissors
Sample Personal Memorial (optional)

Process

Review

1. Ask students whether anyone has had any additional thoughts about funerals or how we remember people who have died. Encourage the group to reiterate the main point of the session: When a person dies, the friends and family may need some kind of special ritual to help them understand that the person is gone and to memorialize them.

Working Time

1. Briefly describe the goals of the session.
2. Discuss the fact that, at a funeral, many people attend. This ritual is therefore public. Point out that it can also be helpful to find private ways to remember a person we have lost.
3. Distribute the art materials and encourage students to create their own personal memorial to help them express their thoughts and feelings about the person who is ill or who has died. They may wish to include some of the following kinds of information:
   - The person's name
   - The person's age (now, if still living, or at time of death)
   - Relationship to the student (grandmother, friend, etc.)
   - Something that person liked to do as a hobby
   - What that person did for a living
   - A special event in that person's life
   - The person's favorite season, food, color, etc.
   - Something the person shared with the student
   - Memorable characteristics (e.g., "He would do anything for you"; "She really enjoyed life")

   Encourage students to be creative in expressing their feelings by drawing pictures, writing poems, and so forth. If desired, you may choose to share as an illustration a personal memorial for someone you yourself have lost.
4. Allow plenty of time at the end of the session for students to show and talk about their personal memorials with the group. The following questions may help guide discussion.
   - What words and images did you choose to help you create your personal memorial? Why were these ideas important?
   - What feelings did you have while you were working on your personal memorial?

- Do you think having this document will help you remember the person?
- How did it feel to share your personal memorial with other members of the group?

Closing Time

1. Ask whether students think it would be worthwhile to start a scrapbook or journal to record more ideas about the person who is ill or who has died. Some of the things they could include would be interviews with other friends or family about the person, photographs, recollections of holidays or other special times together, drawings of the person's house or pets, and so forth. Invite students to brainstorm more ideas about what might be included.
2. Ask whether there is anything anyone would like to say before the group ends and mention the topic of the next session (understanding suicide). Tell students you will be available to them between sessions and remind them of the confidentiality rule and the time for the next session.

Understanding Suicide

Goals

1. To explore the reasons why a death by suicide might be harder for survivors to deal with than other deaths
2. To help students realize that children, adolescents, and adults have different orientations toward suicide
3. To show that suicide is often a permanent solution to a temporary problem and to present the warning signs of suicide
4. To teach students that they must report suicide signs in themselves or in others immediately

Materials

Suicide Warning Signs List

Process

Review

1. Ask whether anyone in the group decided to create a scrapbook or journal to record their thoughts and feelings. If so, what kinds of information did they choose to include? If not, did they have any additional thoughts about the personal memorial they created during the last session? Did they share the memorial with any of their friends or family?

Working Time

1. Briefly describe the goals of the session. [4]
2. Explain that if someone takes his or her own life it can be a devastating time for those left behind. Family and friends may wonder whether there was anything they could have done to stop the person and may feel extremely guilty as a result. Discuss the following questions.
   - Why do you think survivors of a suicide might feel especially guilty?
   - Are the survivors to blame if someone commits suicide?
   - What could these people do to help get over their guilty feelings?
3. Point out that survivors may also be very angry because the person who died actively deprived them of a chance to help, say goodbye, or try to do things differently. Ask students whether they can think of any other reasons survivors might be angry with the person who died (e.g., the person's death seems like a waste, survivors believe suicide is wrong, etc.).
4. Discuss the idea that people at different ages have different orientations toward suicide. Specifically, younger children may commit suicide impulsively, without understanding that death is a permanent state. Adolescents know that death is permanent but because they have limited life experience may feel suicide is the only solution to their problems. (For example, if your boyfriend or girlfriend drops you, you might think that the pain and embarrassment you feel will last forever or that no one will ever love you again.) Stress that suicide is often a permanent solution to a temporary problem and that getting the right kind of help is essential. For instance, if a person is considering suicide because he or she is very depressed, sometimes talking to a counselor or having a doctor prescribe antidepressant drugs can help solve the problem.

[4] If there has been a recent suicide in the school or in students' other acquaintance, this session should be adjusted so group members have sufficient time to work on their feelings about the specific situation. Just listening is important: Let students pour out their pain and confusion in any way they need.

5. Invite students to generate some possible reasons a person might commit suicide. Responses might include the following ideas.
   - Not seeing any reason to keep on living
   - Having unendurable emotional or physical pain
   - Feeling helpless and out of control
   - Feeling unwanted, unloved, or unimportant
   - Wanting to "get even" with someone
   - Wanting to get attention from someone
   - Being afraid to work on problems
   - Feeling like a failure
   - Having too much stress and not being able to cope
   - Losing loved ones (through death, moving away, divorce, etc.) and not being able to come to terms with the feeling of loss
   - Being depressed
6. Distribute the Suicide Warning Signs List and discuss. Point out that having one or two of these feelings on occasion does not necessarily mean someone is on the verge of suicide, but that having a number of them frequently may be serious. In addition, some signs should always be taken seriously—for instance, direct statements indicating that someone is planning suicide.
7. Explain that sometimes these warning signs are ways individuals thinking of suicide communicate to the people around them that they are feeling this way. Some of these ways of communicating are direct (e.g., saying, "I think I'll just end it all"), but sometimes they are indirect (e.g., withdrawing from friends or family). Emphasize the fact that, especially in youth suicide, there is often no external event that "causes" the suicide and that it is important to pay attention to these more subtle signs.
8. Discuss ways students might intervene if they or someone they know is feeling or acting suicidal. Important points to raise are as follows.
   - Don't avoid the situation because it is scary or threatening to talk to a person who might be feeling suicidal.
   - Do ask the person whether he or she is thinking of committing suicide. Asking a direct question will not influence a person to do something he or she has not already considered doing, and it just might help you to know how seriously the person is thinking about suicide.
   - Do share information about the person's feelings with your counselor or another adult (parent or teacher) so the person can get help.
   - Don't try to protect the person by keeping this information a secret.
   - Do ask for help for yourself if you need to sort out your own feelings about the situation.

Closing Time

1. Go around the circle and ask students to tell you what they should do if they notice suicide signs in someone they know or if they feel suicidal themselves. *(Get help immediately.)* Invite students to speak with you privately if they feel they or someone they know has a problem.
2. Ask whether there is anything anyone would like to say before the group ends and mention the topic of the next session (healing ourselves). Tell students you will be available to them between sessions and remind them of the confidentiality rule and the time for the next meeting.

Suicide Warning Signs List

Instructions: If you or someone you know is thinking about suicide or showing a lot of these signs, be sure to get help immediately from your counselor or another adult.

Things a person might do

1. Give away prized possessions
2. Possess or get a weapon such as a knife or gun
3. Make a plan for committing suicide
4. Show sudden mood swings (be very happy after being very depressed)
5. Have attempted suicide before
6. Make a will and put personal affairs in order
7. Be self-destructive physically or in other ways
8. Show a change in eating habits (eating too much or too little)
9. Show belligerent, acting-out, or destructive behavior
10. Neglect to take care of physical appearance
11. Complain about physical problems (e.g., headaches)
12. Get in trouble with the law
13. Break up with a boyfriend or girlfriend
14. Write poems or make drawings about death
15. Drive while drinking
16. Show a drop in grades or have frequent absences from school

Things a person might say

1. Talk openly about committing suicide ("I think I'll just end it all.")
2. Ask questions about suicide (what would it be like, etc.)
3. Talk about not being around in the future
4. Talk about different ways to commit suicide
5. Say things that don't make sense or are confused
6. Say that things that used to be fun aren't fun anymore
7. Talk about revenge, "getting even" with someone
8. Say negative things about self, express self-blame and guilt

Things a person might feel

1. Depression, apathy ("don't care" attitude)
2. Irritability, restlessness, agitation, inability to relax
3. Fatigue, low energy nearly every day
4. Hostility, desire for revenge
5. Indecision
6. Lack of concentration
7. A sense of being a failure or worthlessness
8. Hopelessness, helplessness
9. Dissatisfaction with everything and everyone
10. A sense of being unloved, unwanted, rejected
11. Extreme stress
12. A lack of control
13. A lack of support from any source

Things that might have happened

1. Losing a relative or friend to death, divorce, or moving away
2. Having family problems such as job loss or alcohol/drug abuse
3. Losing money or prestige, having to move to a less desirable house or apartment
4. Failing in a class or being held back a grade in school
5. Having a boyfriend or girlfriend break off a relationship
6. Finding out about a medical illness
7. Experiencing parents' divorce

Healing Ourselves

Goals

1. To help students become aware that there are self-destructive behaviors other than suicide
2. To suggest alternate coping methods for dealing with the deep feelings engendered by loss
3. To help students understand that coming to terms with a loss is a slow process but that they have the power to choose the ways they will accomplish this healing

Materials

Chalkboard or chart paper

Suicide Warning Signs List (from Session 6)

Process

Review

1. Discuss any additional thoughts and feelings students may have as a result of thinking about the Suicide Warning Signs List. Remind students that if they or anyone they know is experiencing these signs, they must report the problem immediately.

Working Time

1. Briefly describe the goals of the session.
2. Point out that suicide is the ultimate self-destruction but that people sometimes do other self-destructive things when they are faced with problems. Invite students to close their eyes and imagine a time when they were really sad, upset, or down.
3. After a minute or so, ask whether anyone would be willing to share such an experience. Discuss, then help the group brainstorm various self-destructive responses students might have made to their problem. (These will likely overlap the responses on the Suicide Warning Signs List.) Write responses on the chalkboard or chart paper under the heading *self-destructive.* Ideas might include the following.
   - Using drugs or alcohol
   - Being sexually irresponsible
   - Isolating yourself from other people
   - Refusing to get help for a physical or psychological problem
   - Denying that anything is wrong if you have a problem
   - Lashing out at other people
   - Allowing your emotions to control your life
   - Being extremely passive or aggressive
   - Refusing to learn more positive coping skills
   - Allowing relationships with others to deteriorate
4. Point out that it takes time to heal from the loss of someone you love, but that choosing more positive ways of coping can help. Have students brainstorm some ways they could help heal themselves. Write these ideas on the chalkboard or chart paper under a column headed *healing.* Responses might include the following.
   - Don't be afraid to be angry at losing someone you love. Find someone to talk to about your anger rather than taking it out on yourself or the people around you.
   - Find a counselor to help you work through your grief. Grieving is a normal process, even though it hurts.
   - Share your feelings with family members. Don't keep them bottled up inside.

- Write a letter to the person who is ill or who has died to say all the things you might not have had a chance to.
- Develop hobbies to gain a sense of expertise and enjoyment.
- Do things for others; volunteer.
- Take care of yourself: Get regular physical exercise and eat a balanced diet.
- Get a pet that you can talk to, care for, and love.

5. Discuss why the more positive coping methods might be better in the long run. Elicit the idea that self-destructive behavior can cause you additional problems that you will just have to solve later and that it won't really help you deal with your loss.

Closing Time

1. Ask students whether they would be willing to try any of these positive ways of coping. Which ones do they think would work best? When do they plan to start?
2. Ask whether there is anything anyone would like to say before the group ends and mention the topic of the final session (reviewing what has been learned in the group and saying goodbye). Tell students you will be available to them between sessions and remind them of the confidentiality rule and the time for the next meeting.

Saying Goodbye

Goals

1. To provide a review of what has happened in the past seven sessions
2. To help students understand and cope with the fact that the group is ending
3. To illustrate the importance of saying goodbye and give students a chance to achieve closure on the group and their relationships in it
4. To provide students with resources for further counseling, if necessary

Materials

List of mental health services for follow-up care (crisis lines, counselors, etc.)

Nutritious snack for everyone (raisins, fruit drink, etc.)

Process

Review

1. Discuss whether students were able to use any of the positive coping methods discussed in the last session. Which ones did they choose? Have they noticed any results from their efforts?
2. Next, go through the session topics and discuss what students feel are the most important lessons they learned in the group. The following questions may be helpful.

   - What are some of the feelings you have had concerning the person who is ill or who has died? What was it like for you to share these feelings in the group? (Session 1)
   - What is the legal definition of death? *(brain waves stop)* How can the causes of death be categorized? *(illness, accident, deliberate action)* What does it mean to say death is part of the natural cycle? (Session 2)
   - What are some of the emotions experienced by people who are dying and by their friends and family? *(denial, isolation, anger, bargaining, depression, acceptance)* (Session 3)
   - Why do you think people have funerals? Do you think having some kind of special ritual is important when someone dies? (Session 4)
   - What is a personal memorial? Did creating a personal memorial help you in any way? (Session 5)
   - What are some of the reasons a person might commit suicide? Is there always a reason? How might a child's or adolescent's reasons be different from those of an adult? What should you do if you or someone you know is feeling suicidal? (Session 6)
   - What are some ways people can be self-destructive besides suicide? What are some more positive coping methods? Which do you choose? (Session 7)

Working Time

1. Point out that all relationships come to an end, whether by moving away or mutual decision, or for other reasons, including death. Encourage students to talk about their own experiences with having relationships end.
2. Discuss the importance of goodbyes, stressing that saying goodbye can help people deal with the sadness they might feel that the group is ending.
3. Invite each student in the group to complete the following sentence stem: "What this group has meant to me is . . . "
4. Share a positive statement about each student. For example: "Stefan, I really appreciate your sharing your feelings about your friend's death with the group" or "Lisa, you've really come up with some very good ways to deal with your sadness about your grandmother's illness." Invite group members to share similar statements.

Closing Time

1. Thank students for participating and remind them of the confidentiality rule. Tell students that, even though the group is ending, you will continue to be available to them (if indeed this is the case). Distribute the list of local mental health services and let students know that these resources are also available to them.
2. Have a "group hug," if the atmosphere seems right, then share the snacks.

Sample Faculty Group Counseling Needs Assessment

Dear Faculty Member:
The counseling staff will be conducting small-group counseling activities during the academic year. We would like to have your input so that we can better meet your needs and the needs of the youth in this school. Please help us provide the best and most appropriate services possible for our school. Each of the following topics represents a major issue to be covered in an eight-session group counseling experience. A counselor or counselor team will lead the group. Please place a checkmark in front of the topics you think are most valuable. Thank you very much!

____ 1. Dealing with a divorce in the family

____ 2. Meeting, making, and keeping friends

____ 3. Learning assertion skills

____ 4. Developing self-esteem

____ 5. Stress management skills

____ 6. Anger management skills

____ 7. Study and test-taking skills

____ 8. Coping with grief and loss

____ 9. Dealing with alcohol/drugs

____ 10. Learning to make better decisions

____ 11. Relaxation skills

____ 12. Surviving cliques

____ 13. Transition to junior high school/high school

____ 14. Getting along with parents

____ 15. Dating, relationships, and sex

____ 16. Getting along with teachers

____ 17. Other ____

____ 18. Other ____

Comments:

Name____ Date__________

Return to____

Sample Student Group Counseling Needs Assessment

Dear Student:

Your school counselors will be providing group counseling experiences for you during the year. Group counseling is a way for 6–8 students to work with a counselor on such topics as learning to manage stress, friendship skills, learning to make better decisions, dealing with divorce in the family, understanding feelings, etc. Please tell us what group topics you would be interested in or that you think we need at our school. Please put a checkmark next to any subject you think would be helpful. Please circle any subject if you would like to have a counselor speak with you about the possibility of being included in a group.

_____ 1. Dealing with a divorce in the family

_____ 2. Meeting, making, and keeping friends

_____ 3. Learning assertion skills

_____ 4. Developing self-esteem

_____ 5. Stress management skills

_____ 6. Anger management skills

_____ 7. Study and test-taking skills

_____ 8. Coping with grief and loss

_____ 9. Dealing with alcohol/drugs

_____ 10. Learning to make better decisions

_____ 11. Relaxation skills

_____ 12. Surviving cliques

_____ 13. Transition to junior high school/high school

_____ 14. Getting along with parents

_____ 15. Dating, relationships, and sex

_____ 16. Getting along with teachers

_____ 17. Other ____

_____ 18. Other ____

Comments:

Sign your name only if you want to be contacted about a group.

Name____ Date______________

Return to____

Sample Letter to School Faculty

Dear Faculty Member:

The counseling staff will soon be starting a series of group counseling experiences for the youngsters in our school. Group counseling has been found to be very helpful in assisting certain youths in learning important personal and social skills. Group leader(s) will work with 6–8 students for eight sessions of approximately 50 minutes each.

It is important to distinguish between *group counseling* and *group guidance.* Group guidance involves sharing information with a large group, such as an entire class. This information can help students make better life decisions about such matters as use of drugs/alcohol, career paths, etc. Group guidance is designed to prevent issues from becoming problems and is something every student needs and deserves on a regular basis. Group counseling, on the other hand, is remedial in nature. It is meant to help those who are already having problems with developmental issues and to prevent such problems from becoming out of hand. In group counseling, small groups are selected by the counselor to receive this service.

Group counseling is not the best choice for every child who has problems. Some youngsters need more intense, individualized help and would best be served by individual counseling or family therapy. For example, a child who is involved in a crisis of some sort would not be an appropriate candidate for group counseling. A youngster who is so shy that he or she cannot interact in a group would also not be suited. And a youngster who is very aggressive or who needs constant attention would not be a good candidate. So, although a student might need help very badly, group counseling might not be the best type of service. If you know of such students, the counseling staff would be happy to assist in finding appropriate help.

The group counseling experiences coming up are on the following topics:

____.

____.

____.

They will meet from ____________________ to ____________________.

If you have students you think could benefit from this experience, please let us know as soon as possible. We will be happy to meet with you and plan how we can cooperate to make this a special learning experience for the youngsters of our school.

Sincerely,

School Counseling Staff

Sample Letter to Parent/Guardian

Dear Parent or Guardian:

During this school year, your school counseling staff will be offering students in need of services the opportunity to participate in group counseling. About 6–8 youths are selected to be in the group.

Group counseling is an excellent way for some students to learn new skills, develop self-confidence, become more aware of how others see them, practice new behaviors, and better understand how to deal with the many problems life presents.

Your child has expressed interest in participating in a group that will be starting soon. Enclosed is a form that asks you to give your consent for your child to participate. He or she has not been selected yet and will not be considered until you give your permission. Only a few students will be able to have this opportunity at a time. If your child is not selected but is an appropriate candidate for future services, he or she will have other opportunities to participate. Participation in the group is completely voluntary and will not affect your child's grades in any way.

Please read the Parent/Guardian Consent Form thoroughly and return it by [date]. If you have questions, concerns, or comments, please call us at the number and time listed below. Thank you very much for considering this opportunity for your child.

Sincerely,

School Counseling Staff

Telephone number____

Best time to call____

Sample Parent/Guardian Consent Form

Your permission is requested for your child [name] to participate in group counseling activities at [school]. The group counseling will run for approximately [number of weeks], from [date] to [date]. A total of [number of sessions] of [number of minutes] each is scheduled. The group is entitled [topic/title] and will include discussion of ideas, behaviors, feelings, attitudes, and opinions. Some of the subjects to be covered in the group are as follows.

____

____

____

Participants will have the opportunity to learn new skills and behaviors that may help their personal development and adjustment. The group will be led by [name(s)], of the school counseling staff.

Because counseling is based on a trusting relationship between counselor and client, the group leader(s) will keep the information shared by group members confidential except in certain situations in which there is an ethical responsibility to limit confidentiality. In the following circumstances, you will be notified.

1. If the child reveals information about hurting himself/herself or another person
2. If the child reveals information about child abuse
3. If the child reveals information about criminal activity
4. Other______________________________

By signing this form I give my informed consent for my child to participate in group counseling. I understand that

1. The group will provide an opportunity for members to learn and practice interpersonal skills, discuss feelings, share ideas, practice new behaviors, and make new friends.
2. Anything group members share in group will be kept confidential by the group leader(s) except in the above-mentioned cases.

Parent/Guardian______________________________ Date__________

Parent/Guardian______________________________ Date__________

Student______________________________ Date__________

Return to______________________________

TAP-In Student Selection Checklist

Date__________ Interviewer____

Name of Student____

Age______ Grade______ Group___________________________________

Tell

_____ 1. The purpose and goals of the group.

_____ 2. Where, when, and how often the group will meet.

_____ 3. The name of the group leader(s).

_____ 4. The number of students to be selected (not everyone who wants to be in the group will be selected).

_____ 5. Both student and parents must give permission.

_____ 6. Members will be expected to share some personal things about themselves, such as ideas, feelings, attitudes, and behaviors, but no one will force you to share anything you do not wish to.

_____ 7. Benefits of being in the group (be specific to group topic).

_____ 8. Risks of being in the group (negative feelings or behaviors from self and others as a result of learning new things or making changes).

_____ 9. In group, we agree to keep whatever is said confidential (no one tells what is said to anyone outside the group). Since none of us has complete control over all of the members, we can't guarantee that another group member will not break your confidence. Also, there are times when the group leader(s) would have to share what you say with other adults, such as your parents.

- If you say you will harm yourself or someone else
- If you tell about a crime you are involved in or know about
- If you tell about child abuse happening to yourself or someone else

_____ 10. All group members are expected to be on time for each meeting. A close bond forms in the group because members are sharing and learning together. It therefore affects everyone when one person is absent.

_____ 11. You may stop being a member of the group at any time, but you need to let the group leader(s) know, not just stop coming.

_____ 12. No physical, verbal, or drug abuse is allowed in group.

_____ 13. Each group member is expected to do some self-improvement exercises between sessions. (These are like "personal homework.")

_____ 14. Each group member is expected to work on behavior change goals.

Ask

_____ 1. Do you understand everything I have said about the group so far?

_____ 2. What else would you like to know about the group? About the leaders?

_____ 3. Are you going to any other counselor or psychologist for counseling outside of school? Any other group counseling?

_____ 4. If chosen for the group, will you attend regularly?

_____ 5. Are you willing to share personal things about yourself, such as your ideas, thoughts, feelings, or behaviors?

_____ 6. Are you willing to do the self-improvement exercises between meetings?

_____ 7. What goals would you like to work toward? (In other words, how do you want to be different at the end of the group?)

_____ 8. Would you give your permission for the leader(s) to audiotape/videotape you during some sessions? (Ask only if applicable.)

_____ 9. On a scale of 1–10, how much do you want to be a member of the group?

Interviewer (signature)____ Date__________

Pick

Note: Complete this part after the interview with the student is finished.

_____ 1. Does this student seem to understand the purpose and goals of the group?

_____ 2. Does this student appear to want to participate and be a productive group member?

_____ 3. Does this student have some positive behaviors from which other members could learn?

_____ 4. Does this student seem compatible with others tentatively selected?

_____ 5. Does this student appear to be making the decision to join the group independently or under the influence of others?

_____ 6. Does this student appear to be giving informed consent?

_____ 7. What is this student's motivation factor (scale of 1–10)?

Selected_____ Not Selected_____

Potential for Future Group? Yes _____ No _____

Comments:

Pretests/Posttests

Name______________________________ Date______________

Dealing with a Divorce in the Family

Instructions: Each of the statements below concerns your ideas, beliefs, attitudes, or feelings about divorce. After each statement is a response you could choose. Circle the response that is how you think or feel now.

Scale 1 = never
2 = hardly ever
3 = sometimes
4 = most of the time
5 = always

Example: I like to eat chips and drink pop. *You hardly ever like to eat chips and drink pop.*	1	(2)	3	4	5
1. I think people who get married should never get divorced.	1	2	3	4	5
2. I can talk about the divorce with my parents, and they will listen to me.	1	2	3	4	5
3. I have a support system of friends who understand me.	1	2	3	4	5
4. I can express my feelings about the divorce.	1	2	3	4	5
5. I like visiting the parent I don't live with.	1	2	3	4	5
6. I feel comfortable asking for what I want and need.	1	2	3	4	5
7. Ending relationships is very scary to me.	1	2	3	4	5
8. I feel as though I don't have any control over what is happening at home.	1	2	3	4	5
9. I think it is better to get my feelings out than it is to keep them inside.	1	2	3	4	5
10. I think I can learn to deal with my problems.	1	2	3	4	5

Name____ Date__________________

Meeting, Making, and Keeping Friends

Instructions: Each of the statements below concerns your ideas, beliefs, attitudes, or feelings about friendships. After each statement is a response you could choose. Circle the response that is how you think or feel now.

Scale 1 = never
2 = hardly ever
3 = sometimes
4 = most of the time
5 = always

Example: I like to watch TV in the evening.	1	2	(3)	4	5
You like to watch TV in the evening sometimes.					
1. I enjoy meeting new kids my age.	1	2	3	4	5
2. I worry about meeting new friends.	1	2	3	4	5
3. I would like to have many friends.	1	2	3	4	5
4. I know how to tell my friends how I feel.	1	2	3	4	5
5. I can talk about what is important to me with friends.	1	2	3	4	5
6. I have trouble expressing negative feelings (like anger or sadness).	1	2	3	4	5
7. I have trouble keeping friends for more than a few weeks.	1	2	3	4	5
8. I am loyal to my friends.	1	2	3	4	5
9. I know why my friendships end.	1	2	3	4	5
10. I don't like what my friends do, but I go along anyway.	1	2	3	4	5

Name____ Date____________________

Communicate Straight: Learning Assertion Skills

Instructions: Each of the statements below concerns your ideas, beliefs, attitudes, or feelings about being assertive. After each statement is a response you could choose. Circle the response that is how you think or feel now.

Scale 1 = never
2 = hardly ever
3 = sometimes
4 = most of the time
5 = always

Example: I like to watch TV in the evening. *You hardly ever like to watch TV in the evening.*	1	(2)	3	4	5
1. I enjoy meeting new kids my age.	1	2	3	4	5
2. I let other kids boss me around.	1	2	3	4	5
3. I'm honest about my feelings with my close friends.	1	2	3	4	5
4. I have a right to express my feelings to my parents.	1	2	3	4	5
5. I have a right to ask for what I need.	1	2	3	4	5
6. A person can change how he or she gets along with others.	1	2	3	4	5
7. I have trouble expressing negative feelings like anger.	1	2	3	4	5
8. I can't talk to my parents about what I want.	1	2	3	4	5
9. I feel as though I have to go along or I won't have any friends.	1	2	3	4	5
10. I have a right to say no to things I don't want to do.	1	2	3	4	5

Name____ Date____________________

Feeling Good about Me: Developing Self-esteem

Instructions: Each of the statements below concerns your ideas, beliefs, attitudes, or feelings about yourself. After each statement is a response you could choose. Circle the response that is how you think or feel now.

Scale 1 = never
2 = hardly ever
3 = sometimes
4 = most of the time
5 = always

Example: I like to choose my own clothes.	1	2	3	4	⑤
You always like to choose your own clothes.					
1. I feel good about myself.	1	2	3	4	5
2. I understand my feelings.	1	2	3	4	5
3. I know what others think of me.	1	2	3	4	5
4. I am a good student.	1	2	3	4	5
5. My teachers seem to like me.	1	2	3	4	5
6. My parents are pleased with how I am doing in school.	1	2	3	4	5
7. Other kids want me to be their friend.	1	2	3	4	5
8. I feel as though I fit in at school.	1	2	3	4	5
9. I feel as though I am a successful person so far in my life.	1	2	3	4	5
10. I believe I have a good future ahead of me.	1	2	3	4	5

Name____ Date____________________

Keeping Your Cool: Stress Management Skills

Instructions: Each of the statements below concerns your ideas, beliefs, attitudes, or feelings about stress and stressful situations. After each statement is a response you could choose. Circle the response that is how you think or feel now.

Scale 1 = never
2 = hardly ever
3 = sometimes
4 = most of the time
5 = always

Example: I like to watch TV in the evenings. 1 2 3 (4) 5

You like to watch TV in the evenings most of the time.

1. I feel as though I am in control of my life.	1	2	3	4	5
2. I understand what causes me stress.	1	2	3	4	5
3. There is too much going on in my life.	1	2	3	4	5
4. I know how I react to stress.	1	2	3	4	5
5. When things get too much for me, I do something I usually regret.	1	2	3	4	5
6. I know how to relax.	1	2	3	4	5
7. I don't know what to do when I get stressed out.	1	2	3	4	5
8. I feel anxious at school.	1	2	3	4	5
9. I feel anxious at home.	1	2	3	4	5
10. I feel anxious when I am with my friends.	1	2	3	4	5

Name______________________________ Date______________

Better Ways of Getting Mad: Anger Management Skills

Instructions: Each of the statements below concerns your ideas, beliefs, attitudes, or feelings about anger. After each statement is a response you could choose. Circle the response that is how you think or feel now.

Scale 1 = never
2 = hardly ever
3 = sometimes
4 = most of the time
5 = always

Example: I like to eat hamburgers and fries. *You hardly ever like to eat hamburgers and fries.*	1	(2)	3	4	5
1. I know what makes me mad.	1	2	3	4	5
2. I understand my angry feelings.	1	2	3	4	5
3. I believe that my anger is the cause of my problems.	1	2	3	4	5
4. I just can't control my anger.	1	2	3	4	5
5. I think anger is a bad thing.	1	2	3	4	5
6. When I am angry, I express my feelings to the person I am angry with.	1	2	3	4	5
7. Other people cause my anger.	1	2	3	4	5
8. I wish I could express anger better.	1	2	3	4	5
9. I am responsible for my own anger.	1	2	3	4	5
10. I know what kinds of situations get me angry.	1	2	3	4	5

Name____ Date____________________

School Survival and Success

Instructions: Each of the statements below concerns your ideas, beliefs, attitudes, or feelings about how you get along at school. After each statement is a response you could choose. Circle the response that is how you think or feel now.

Scale 1 = never
2 = hardly ever
3 = sometimes
4 = most of the time
5 = always

Example: Lunch is my favorite class period. 1 2 3 (4) 5

Lunch is your favorite class period most of the time.

1. I am able to manage my time.	1	2	3	4	5
2. I know what my goals for school are.	1	2	3	4	5
3. I don't feel as though I am getting the most out of class.	1	2	3	4	5
4. Decision making is hard for me.	1	2	3	4	5
5. I let other kids take advantage of me.	1	2	3	4	5
6. I ask for what I want and need.	1	2	3	4	5
7. I know how to study for a test.	1	2	3	4	5
8. I give in to pressure from others to do things I don't want to do.	1	2	3	4	5
9. I feel stressed-out at school.	1	2	3	4	5
10. I can control my stress.	1	2	3	4	5

Name____ Date____________________

Coping with Grief and Loss

Instructions: Each of the statements below concerns your ideas, beliefs, or feelings about grief and loss. After each statement is a response you could choose. Circle the response that is how you think or feel now.

Scale
1 = never
2 = hardly ever
3 = sometimes
4 = most of the time
5 = always

Example: I enjoy staying up past 9:00 p.m. on weekends. 1 2 3 (4) 5

You enjoy staying up past 9:00 p.m. on weekends most of the time.

1. It is scary to think about dying.	1	2	3	4	5
2. It is all right to cry when someone dies.	1	2	3	4	5
3. I understand what death is.	1	2	3	4	5
4. I think it is important to go to funerals.	1	2	3	4	5
5. I would want to know the truth about someone in my family who was dying.	1	2	3	4	5
6. It is important to tell an adult when you hear someone talking about committing suicide.	1	2	3	4	5
7. I can think of some reasons why someone might want to take his or her own life.	1	2	3	4	5
8. Sometimes I think about taking my own life.	1	2	3	4	5
9. Parents should talk openly and honestly about dying in front of their kids.	1	2	3	4	5
10. Learning more about death, dying, and loss would be helpful to me.	1	2	3	4	5

Ethical Guidelines for Group Counselors

Preamble

One characteristic of any professional group is the possession of a body of knowledge, skills, and voluntarily self-professed standards for ethical practice.* A Code of Ethics consists of those standards that have been formally and publicly acknowledged by the members of a profession to serve as the guidelines for professional conduct, discharge of duties, and the resolution of moral dilemmas. By this document, the Association for Specialists in Group Work (ASGW) has identified the standards of conduct appropriate for ethical behavior among its members.

ASGW recognizes the basic commitment of its members to the Ethical Standards of its parent organization, the American Association for Counseling and Development (AACD) and nothing in this document shall be construed to supplant that code. These standards are intended to complement AACD standards in the area of group work by clarifying the nature of ethical responsibility of the counselor in the group setting and by stimulating a greater concern for competent group leadership.

The group counselor is expected to be a professional agent and to take the processes of ethical responsibility seriously. ASGW views "ethical process" as being integral to group work and views group counselors as "ethical agents." Group counselors, by their very nature in being responsible and responsive to their group members, necessarily embrace a certain potential for ethical vulnerability. It is incumbent upon group counselors to give considerable attention to the intent and context of their actions because the attempts of counselors to influence human behavior through group work always have ethical implications.

The following ethical guidelines have been developed to encourage ethical behavior of group counselors. These guidelines are written for students and practitioners, and are meant to stimulate reflection, self-examination, and discussion of issues and practices. They address the group counselor's responsibility for providing information about group work to clients and the group counselor's responsibility for providing group counseling services to clients. A final section discusses the group counselor's responsibility for safeguarding ethical practice and procedures for reporting unethical behavior. Group counselors are expected to make known these standards to group members.

Ethical Guidelines

1. Orientation and Providing Information:

   Group counselors adequately prepare prospective or new group members by providing as much information about the existing or proposed group as necessary.

   Minimally, information related to each of the following areas should be provided.

   (a) Entrance procedures, time parameters of the group experience, group participation expectations, methods of payment (where appropriate), and termination procedures are explained by the group counselor as appropriate to the level of maturity of group members and the nature and purpose(s) of the group.

   (b) Group counselors have available for distribution a professional disclosure statement that includes information on the group counselor's qualifications and group services that can be provided, particularly as related to the nature and purpose(s) of the specific group.

   (c) Group counselors communicate the role expectations, rights, and responsibilities of group members and group counselor(s).

   (d) The group goals are stated as concisely as possible by the group counselor, including "whose" goal it is (the group counselor's, the institution's, the parent's, the law's, society's, etc.) and the role of group members in influencing or determining the group's goal(s).

   (e) Group counselors explore with group members the risks of potential life changes that may occur because of the group experience and help members explore their readiness to face these possibilities.

* These guidelines, drafted June 1, 1989, by the Association for Specialists in Group Work (ASGW), have been reprinted by permission of the American Association for Counseling and Development (AACD), 5999 Stevenson Avenue, Alexandria, VA 22304.

(f) Group members are informed by the group counselor of unusual or experimental procedures that might be expected in their group experience.

(g) Group counselors explain, as realistically as possible, what services can and cannot be provided within the particular group structure offered.

(h) Group counselors emphasize the need to promote full psychological functioning and presence among group members. They inquire from prospective group members whether they are using any kind of drug or medication that may affect functioning in the group. They do not permit any use of alcohol and/or illegal drugs during group sessions and they discourage the use of alcohol and/or drugs (legal or illegal) prior to group meetings which may affect the physical or emotional presence of the member or other group members.

(i) Group counselors inquire from prospective group members whether they have ever been a client in counseling or psychotherapy. If a prospective group member is already in a counseling relationship with another professional person, the group counselor advises the prospective group member to notify the other professional of their participation in the group.

(j) Group counselors clearly inform group members about the policies pertaining to the group counselor's willingness to consult with them between group sessions.

(k) In establishing fees for group counseling services, group counselors consider the financial status and the locality of prospective group members. Group members are not charged fees for group sessions where the group counselor is not present and the policy of charging for sessions missed by a group member is clearly communicated. Fees for participating as a group member are contracted between group counselor and group member for a specified period of time. Group counselors do not increase fees for group counseling services until the existing contracted fee structure has expired. In the event that the established fee structure is inappropriate for a prospective member, group counselors assist in finding comparable services of acceptable cost.

2. Screening of Members: The group counselor screens prospective group members (when appropriate to their theoretical orientation). Insofar as possible, the counselor selects group members whose needs and goals are compatible with the goals of the group, who will not impede the group process, and whose well-being will not be jeopardized by the group experience. An orientation to the group (i.e., ASGW Ethical Guideline #1), is included during the screening process.

   Screening may be accomplished in one or more ways, such as the following:

   (a) Individual interview,

   (b) Group interview of prospective group members,

   (c) Interview as part of a team staffing, and

   (d) Completion of a written questionnaire by prospective group members.

3. Confidentiality: Group counselors protect members by defining clearly what confidentiality means, why it is important, and the difficulties involved in enforcement.

   (a) Group counselors take steps to protect members by defining confidentiality and the limits of confidentiality (i.e., when a group member's condition indicates that there is clear and imminent danger to the member, others, or physical property, the group counselor takes reasonable personal action and/or informs responsible authorities).

   (b) Group counselors stress the importance of confidentiality and set a norm of confidentiality regarding all group participants' disclosures. The importance of maintaining confidentiality is emphasized before the group begins and at various times in the group. The fact that confidentiality cannot be guaranteed is clearly stated.

   (c) Members are made aware of the difficulties involved in enforcing and ensuring confidentiality in a group setting. The counselor provides examples of how confidentiality can non-maliciously be broken to increase members' awareness, and helps to lessen the likelihood that this breach of confidence will occur. Group counselors inform group members about the potential consequences of intentionally breaching confidentiality.

(d) Group counselors can only ensure confidentiality on their part and not on the part of the members.

(e) Group counselors video or audio tape a group session only with the prior consent and the members' knowledge of how the tape will be used.

(f) When working with minors, the group counselor specifies the limits of confidentiality.

(g) Participants in a mandatory group are made aware of any reporting procedures required of the group counselor.

(h) Group counselors store or dispose of group member records (written, audio, video, etc.) in ways that maintain confidentiality.

(i) Instructors of group counseling courses maintain the anonymity of group members whenever discussing group counseling cases.

4. Voluntary/Involuntary Participation: Group counselors inform members whether participation is voluntary or involuntary.

(a) Group counselors take steps to ensure informed consent procedures in both voluntary and involuntary groups.

(b) When working with minors in a group, counselors are expected to follow the procedures specified by the institution in which they are practicing.

(c) With involuntary groups, every attempt is made to enlist the cooperation of the members and their continuance in the group on a voluntary basis.

(d) Group counselors do not certify that group treatment has been received by members who merely attend sessions, but did not meet the defined group expectations. Group members are informed about the consequences for failing to participate in a group.

5. Leaving a Group: Provisions are made to assist a group member to terminate in an effective way.

(a) Procedures to be followed for a group member who chooses to exit a group prematurely are discussed by the counselor with all group members either before the group begins, during a pre-screening interview, or during the initial group session.

(b) In the case of legally mandated group counseling, group counselors inform members of the possible consequences for premature self-termination.

(c) Ideally, both the group counselor and the member can work cooperatively to determine the degree to which a group experience is productive or counter-productive for that individual.

(d) Members ultimately have a right to discontinue membership in the group, at a designated time, if the predetermined trial period proves to be unsatisfactory.

(e) Members have the right to exit a group, but it is important that they be made aware of the importance of informing the counselor and the group members prior to deciding to leave. The counselor discusses the possible risks of leaving the group prematurely with a member who is considering this option.

(f) Before leaving a group, the group counselor encourages members (if appropriate) to discuss their reasons for wanting to discontinue membership in the group. Counselors intervene if other members use undue pressure to force a member to remain in the group.

6. Coercion and Pressure: Group counselors protect member rights against physical threats, intimidation, coercion, and undue peer pressure insofar as is reasonably possible.

(a) It is essential to differentiate between "therapeutic pressure" that is part of any group and "undue pressure," which is not therapeutic.

(b) The purpose of a group is to help participants find their own answer, not to pressure them into doing what the group thinks is appropriate.

(c) Counselors exert care not to coerce participants to change in directions which they clearly state they do not choose.

(d) Counselors have a responsibility to intervene when others use undue pressure or attempt to persuade members against their will.

(e) Counselors intervene when any member attempts to act out aggression in a physical way that might harm another member or themselves.

(f) Counselors intervene when a member is verbally abusive or inappropriately confrontive to another member.

7. Imposing Counselor Values: Group counselors develop an awareness of their own values and needs and the potential impact they have on the interventions likely to be made.
   (a) Although group counselors take care to avoid imposing their values on members, it is appropriate that they expose their own beliefs, decisions, needs, and values, when concealing them would create problems for the members.
   (b) There are values implicit in any group, and these are made clear to potential members before they join the group. (Examples of certain values include: expressing feelings, being direct and honest, sharing personal material with others, learning how to trust, improving interpersonal communication, and deciding for oneself.)
   (c) Personal and professional needs of group counselors are not met at the members' expense.
   (d) Group counselors avoid using the group for their own therapy.
   (e) Group counselors are aware of their own values and assumptions and how these apply in a multicultural context.
   (f) Group counselors take steps to increase their awareness of ways that their personal reactions to members might inhibit the group process and they monitor their countertransference. Through an awareness of the impact of stereotyping and discrimination (i.e., biases based on age, disability, ethnicity, gender, race, religion, or sexual preference), group counselors guard the individual rights and personal dignity of all group members.

8. Equitable Treatment: Group counselors make every reasonable effort to treat each member individually and equally.
   (a) Group counselors recognize and respect differences (e.g., cultural, racial, religious, lifestyle, age, disability, gender) among group members.
   (b) Group counselors maintain an awareness of their behavior toward individual group members and are alert to the potential detrimental effects of favoritism or partiality toward any particular group member to the exclusion or detriment of any other member(s). It is likely that group counselors will favor some members over others, yet all group members deserve to be treated equally.
   (c) Group counselors ensure equitable use of group time for each member by inviting silent members to become involved, acknowledging nonverbal attempts to communicate, and discouraging rambling and monopolizing of time by members.
   (d) If a large group is planned, counselors consider enlisting another qualified professional to serve as a co-leader for the group sessions.

9. Dual Relationships: Group counselors avoid dual relationships with group members that might impair their objectivity and professional judgment, as well as those which are likely to compromise a group member's ability to participate fully in the group.
   (a) Group counselors do not misuse their professional role and power as group leader to advance personal or social contacts with members throughout the duration of the group.
   (b) Group counselors do not use their professional relationship with group members to further their own interest either during the group or after the termination of the group.
   (c) Sexual intimacies between group counselors and members are unethical.
   (d) Group counselors do not barter (exchange) professional services with group members for services.
   (e) Group counselors do not admit their own family members, relatives, employees, or personal friends as members to their groups.
   (f) Group counselors discuss with group members the potential detrimental effects of group members engaging in intimate inter-member relationships outside of the group.
   (g) Students who participate in a group as a partial course requirement for a group course are not evaluated for an academic grade based upon their degree of participation as a member in a group. Instructors of group counseling courses take steps to minimize the possible negative impact on students when they participate in a group course by separating course grades from participation in the group and by allowing students to decide what issues to explore and when to stop.

(h) It is inappropriate to solicit members from a class (or institutional affiliation) for one's private counseling or therapeutic groups.

10. Use of Techniques: Group counselors do not attempt any technique unless trained in its use or under supervision by a counselor familiar with the intervention.

    (a) Group counselors are able to articulate a theoretical orientation that guides their practice, and they are able to provide a rationale for their interventions.

    (b) Depending upon the type of an intervention, group counselors have training commensurate with the potential impact of a technique.

    (c) Group counselors are aware of the necessity to modify their techniques to fit the unique needs of various cultural and ethnic groups.

    (d) Group counselors assist members in translating in-group learnings to daily life.

11. Goal Development: Group counselors make every effort to assist members in developing their personal goals.

    (a) Group counselors use their skills to assist members in making their goals specific so that others present in the group will understand the nature of the goals.

    (b) Throughout the course of a group, group counselors assist members in assessing the degree to which personal goals are being met, and assist in revising any goals when it is appropriate.

    (c) Group counselors help members clarify the degree to which the goals can be met within the context of a particular group.

12. Consultation: Group counselors develop and explain policies about between-session consultation to group members.

    (a) Group counselors take care to make certain that members do not use between-session consultations to avoid dealing with issues pertaining to the group that would be dealt with best in the group.

    (b) Group counselors urge members to bring the issues discussed during between-session consultations into the group if they pertain to the group.

    (c) Group counselors seek out consultation and/or supervision regarding ethical concerns or when encountering difficulties which interfere with their effective functioning as group leaders.

    (d) Group counselors seek appropriate professional assistance for their own personal problems or conflicts that are likely to impair their professional judgment and work performance.

    (e) Group counselors discuss their group cases only for professional consultation and educational purposes.

    (f) Group counselors inform members about policies regarding whether consultations will be held confidential.

13. Termination from the Group: Depending upon the purpose of participation in the group, counselors promote termination of members from the group in the most efficient period of time.

    (a) Group counselors maintain a constant awareness of the progress made by each group member and periodically invite the group members to explore and reevaluate their experiences in the group. It is the responsibility of group counselors to help promote the independence of members from the group in a timely manner.

14. Evaluation and Follow-up: Group counselors make every attempt to engage in ongoing assessment and to design follow-up procedures for their groups.

    (a) Group counselors recognize the importance of ongoing assessment of a group, and they assist members in evaluating their own progress.

    (b) Group counselors conduct evaluation of the total group experience at the final meeting (or before termination), as well as ongoing evaluation.

    (c) Group counselors monitor their own behavior and become aware of what they are modeling in the group.

    (d) Follow-up procedures might take the form of personal contact, telephone contact, or written contact.

    (e) Follow-up meetings might be with individuals, or groups, or both to determine the degree to which:
    (i) members have reached their goals,
    (ii) the group had a positive or negative effect on the participants,
    (iii) members could profit from some

type of referral, and (iv) as information for possible modification of future groups. If there is no follow-up meeting, provisions are made available for individual follow-up meetings to any member who needs or requests such a contact.

15. Referrals: If the needs of a particular member cannot be met within the type of group being offered, the group counselor suggests other appropriate professional referrals.
    (a) Group counselors are knowledgeable of local community resources for assisting group members regarding professional referrals.
    (b) Group counselors help members seek further professional assistance, if needed.

16. Professional Development: Group counselors recognize that professional growth is a continuous, ongoing, developmental process throughout their career.
    (a) Group counselors maintain and upgrade their knowledge and skill competencies through educational activities, clinical experiences, and participation in professional development activities.
    (b) Group counselors keep abreast of research findings and new developments as applied to groups.

Safeguarding Ethical Practice and Procedures for Reporting Unethical Behavior

The preceding remarks have been advanced as guidelines which are generally representative of ethical and professional group practice. They have not been proposed as rigidly defined prescriptions. However, practitioners who are thought to be grossly unresponsive to the ethical concerns addressed in this document may be subject to a review of their practices by the AACD Ethics Committee and ASGW peers.

For consultation and/or questions regarding these ASGW Ethical Guidelines or group ethical dilemmas, you may contact the Chairperson of the ASGW Ethics Committee. The name, address, and telephone number of the current ASGW Ethics Committee Chairperson may be acquired by telephoning the AACD office in Alexandria, Virginia at (703) 823-9800.

If a group counselor's behavior is suspected as being unethical, the following procedures are to be followed:

1. Collect more information and investigate further to confirm the unethical practice as determined by the ASGW Ethical Guidelines.

2. Confront the individual with the apparent violation of ethical guidelines for the purposes of protecting the safety of any clients and to help the group counselor correct any inappropriate behaviors. If satisfactory resolution is not reached through this contact then:

3. A complaint should be made in writing, including the specific facts and dates of the alleged violation and all relevant supporting data. The complaint should be included in an envelope marked "CONFIDENTIAL" to ensure confidentiality for both the accuser(s) and the alleged violator(s) and forwarded to all of the following sources:
    (a) The name and address of the Chairperson of the state Counselor Licensure Board for the respective state, if in existence.
    (b) The Ethics Committee

        c/o The President
American Association for Counseling and Development
5999 Stevenson Avenue
Alexandria, Virginia 22304

    (c) The name and address of all private credentialing agencies in which the alleged violator maintains credentials or holds professional membership. Some of these include the following:

        National Board for Certified Counselors, Inc.
5999 Stevenson Avenue
Alexandria, Virginia 22304

        National Council for Credentialing of Career Counselors
c/o NBCC
5999 Stevenson Avenue
Alexandria, Virginia 22304

        National Academy for Certified Clinical Mental Health Counselors
5999 Stevenson Avenue
Alexandria, Virginia 22304

        Commission on Rehabilitation Counselor Certification
162 North State Street, Suite 317
Chicago, Illinois 60601

American Association for Marriage
and Family Therapy
1717 K Street, NW, Suite 407
Washington, DC 20006

American Psychological Association
1200 Seventeenth Street, NW
Washington, DC 20036

American Group Psychotherapy
Association, Inc.
25 East 21st Street, 6th Floor
New York, New York 10010

About the Author

Rosemarie S. Morganett, Ed.D., is an associate professor and Coordinator of Counselor Education at Indiana University Southeast, New Albany, Indiana. Dr. Morganett has been active in leading group counseling experiences in school and mental health settings for over 20 years. Her workshops, training seminars, and group leadership demonstrations have been presented at national, state, and local conventions and conferences. She has been a consultant to school districts, counseling and guidance departments, and state agencies in the area of group counseling and development of counseling programs.

Dr. Morganett holds a doctorate in counseling psychology from Auburn University and is a Clinical Member of the American Association for Marriage and Family Therapists. Her professional interests are in counselor education and promoting group counseling, and her research efforts are in the area of group counseling with youth under stress. She has developed a training manual for counseling laboratories and a structured manual for counseling practica.